Pelican Books
Bandits

Eric J. Hobsbawm was born on 9 June 1917. He was
educated at Vienna, Berlin, London and Cambridge,
where he was a Fellow of King's College from 1949
to 1955. At present he is Professor of Economic
and Social History at Birkbeck College, University
of London, having also taught at Stanford and
Massachusetts Institute of Technology. His main
publications include: *Primitive Rebels* (1959), *The
Age of Revolution* (1962), *Labouring Men* (1964),
*Captain Swing* (1969; with George Rude), and *The
Jazz Scene* (as Francis Newton), and *Industry and
Empire* (Pelican 1969). Professor Hobsbawm, who
lives in London, is married, with two children.

E. J. Hobsbawm

# Bandits

Penguin Books

Penguin Books Ltd, Harmondsworth,
Middlesex, England
Penguin Books Australia Ltd, Ringwood,
Victoria, Australia

First published by Weidenfeld and Nicolson 1969
Published in Pelican Books 1972

Made and printed in Great Britain by
Richard Clay (The Chaucer Press), Ltd
Bungay, Suffolk
Set in Linotype Times

# Contents

# Illustrations

*Illustration Sections*

Engraving of a *bandolero* by John Haynes Williams (1836–1908) (Radio Times Hulton Picture Library)

Nineteenth-century Sicilian theatre puppets (Antonino Uccello)

Popular view of banditry in Catalonia: ex-voto from Ripoll, Gerona province (Ampliaciones y Reproducciones MAS, Barcelona)

Sicilian terracotta group, probably by F. Bonnano (Museo Nazionale di Palazzo Bellomo, Syracuse)

Sicilian peasant wood carving from Syracuse province, mid-nineteenth century (Museo Nazionale di Palazzo Bellomo, Syracuse)

Giuseppe Musolino

Still from De Seta's film *Banditi ad Orgosolo* (National Film Archive)

The brigand romanticized by Charles-Alphonse-Paul Bellay (1826–1900) (Radio Times Hulton Picture Library)

Photograph of Salvatore Giuliano alive (Keystone Press)

Photograph of Salvatore Giuliano dead, 5 July 1950 (Keystone Press)

An ambush by Giuliano's gang reconstructed in Francesco de Rosi's film *Salvatore Giuliano* (National Film Archive)

Posters of bandits wanted by the police in Sardinia (Camera Press)

THE AMERICAS

The James boys as heroes of popular fiction, 1892 (Mansell Collection)

Jesse James (British Museum)

Henry Fonda in the film *Jesse James*, 1939 (National Film Archive)

Title-page of *A Vida de Lampião*, 1962 (Editora Oratica Sonza, São Paolo)

Still from the Brazilian film *O Cangaçeiro*, 1953 (National Film Archive)

'Pancho' Villa as revolutionary general, December 1913 (Radio Times Hulton Picture Library)

Painting by Goya (Ampliaciones y Reproducciones MAS, Barcelona)

*Bandit of the Apennines*, 1824, by Sir Charles Eastlake (Radio Times Hulton Picture Library)

*Brigands*, by Jean-Baptiste Thomas (1781–1854) (Radio Times Hulton Picture Library)

*The Brigand Betrayed*, by Jean-Emile-Horace Vernet (1789–1863) (Wallace Collection)

*Ned Kelly*, 1956, by Sidney Nolan (Arts Council of Great Britain)

*Line Drawings*

The death of 'Vardarelli' of Apulia, engraving, 1833 (British Museum)

Chinese pirate, from *Banditi and Robbers*, 1833 (British Museum)

Three heroes of the Robin Hood cycle in the seventeenth-century Roxburghe Ballads (British Museum)

Autograph of Musolino

'Robin Hood's Chase', from the Roxburghe Ballads (British Museum)

Engraving of Robert Mandrin (Roger-Viollet, Paris)

Bulgarian haiduks, from *La Bulgarie Danubienne*, 1883 (British Museum)

Nineteenth-century engraving of a brigand chief (Radio Times Hulton Picture Library)

Italian bandits 'sharing the loot', engraving (Mansell Collection)

Contemporary engraving of the public execution of Mandrin (Roger-Viollet, Paris)

Contemporary impression of Ned Kelly (Radio Times Hulton Picture Library)

Picture research: Georgina Brückner

# Preface

Except for chapter eight, which is based on first-hand research, most of this book rests on published material, though some of it is rather hard to come by. For the numerous countries whose languages I do not read or whose publications were inaccessible to me, I am also indebted for information, extracted or more likely volunteered with enthusiasm, by friends and colleagues aware of my interest in this subject. This applies to many of my references to banditry in Bulgaria, Greece, Hungary, Russia, Turkey and Tunisia, but also to some of what is written here about various countries of Latin America, the Indian subcontinent, Italy and Spain. My thanks to these learned *aficionados* of Robin Hood and to numerous seminars in Britain and the U.S.A. which criticized the arguments of this book and put me in the way of further sources. My thanks also to the Widener Library of Harvard University, as good a place as I know for the researcher to work in. My particular debts are acknowledged in footnotes, which I have kept to a minimum, the bibliography, and at the end of this preface. A special word of thanks to Enzo Crea of Rome, to M. Antoine Tellez of Paris, and to Sergeant José Avalos of Pampa Grande, Chaco, Argentina, farmer and formerly rural policeman, whose reminiscences of the bandits of Corrientes and the Chaco, whom he respected and pursued, confirm the analysis of Chapter three on almost all points. I can only regret that I did not make his acquaintance until after the text of this book was complete.

Two brief methodological notes: First, it will be clear that I have tried to explain why social banditry is so remarkably uniform a phenomenon throughout the ages and continents. Can this explanation be tested? Yes, in so far as it predicts, broadly speaking, how bandits will act and what stories people will tell about them in areas hitherto unstudied. The present essay elaborates the 'model' originally sketched out in my *Primitive*

*Rebels*, which was based exclusively on European – mostly Spanish and Italian – material, but does not, I hope, conflict with it. Still, the wider the generalization, the more likely it is that individual peculiarities are neglected.

Second, I have relied largely on a rather tricky historical source, namely poems and ballads. So far as the facts of banditry are concerned, these records of public memory and myth are of course quite unreliable, however remotely based on real events, though they give much incidental information about the social environment of banditry, at least in so far as there is no reason why this should be distorted. But there is a more serious difficulty. How far does the 'myth' of banditry throw light on the real pattern of bandit behaviour? In other words, how far do bandits live up to the social role they have been assigned in the drama of peasant life? There is plainly some connection. I hope that in formulating it I have not gone beyond the bounds of common sense.

The above observations are really addressed to the sociologists and social historians who have begun to take a lively interest in bandits. However, I hope this book is not addressed only to them, but can be read and looked at with pleasure and profit by all who share the view expressed by Charles Macfarlane, an earlier writer on this subject, in words which may stand as its epigraph: 'There are few subjects that interest us more generally than the adventures of robbers and *banditi*.'[1]

For help in procuring and identifying illustrations, I am indebted in addition to Prof. B. Cvetkova of Sofia, C. A. Curwen of the School of Oriental and African Studies, Mrs Fei-ling Blackburn and Richard Rogers, and to Mrs Georgina Brückner.

*London, June 1969*                 E. J. HOBSBAWM

# Preface to the Penguin Edition

The present edition has been slightly amplified and changed, but the argument remains substantially unaffected. The one major criticism that has been made of it (by Anton Blok) does not convince me. He argues that the 'noble bandit' or Robin Hood is almost wholly mythical, and reflects not how social bandits really act, but how the common people would like them, or *someone*, to act. Real bandits, it is claimed, victimize peasants as much as anyone else. It is undoubtedly true that Robin Hood characteristics are ascribed to villains who deserve no sympathy whatever, such as Johann Georg Grasel (executed Vienna 1818) an underworld criminal who operated in the north-west of Lower Austria. My friend Georg Eisler has drawn my attention to him. However, there seems to me to be sufficient evidence for genuine Robin Hood behaviour by at least some bandits, and careful readers of this book will observe that I have not claimed that 'noble bandits' are common.

Additional material comes mainly from Latin America. However, friendly readers have supplied me with other suggestions and references, which help to fill out the picture. Carlo Canteri has drawn my attention to the bandits of Tasmania in the early nineteenth century, escaped convicts living on the margins of convict society. George Parsons of Melbourne mentions an urban equivalent of social banditry, Darcy Dugan who was in 1970 under arrest for bank robbery.

He writes,

In the 1950s Dugan achieved the status, almost, of a social bandit. He was arrested on a number of hold-up charges, most of which crimes, the Australian working class believed, had been committed by other criminals whom the police could or would not arrest. Dugan had a reputation for generosity and was viewed, in Sydney at least, in Robin Hood terms . . . I remember an old-timer in a harbour-side pub telling me that 'Darcy was a real gentleman, and they wanted him out of the way because he was a socialist protesting about capitalism. Murderers they understood, but not blokes like Darcy mate, they are revolutionaries.' When he was released in 1967 it appears that he became a social worker in a tough neighbourhood, where his reputation made him rather successful at the job. One may compare the reputation of another urban robber who established, in this instance, a nation-wide fame as a 'noble bandit', Jesus Arriaga, 'Chucho El Roto', of Mexico, who is credited by the author of pulp-fiction with 'the socialist theories which inspired his programme of revenge and struggle'.[2]

Richard Rathbone of the School of Oriental and African Studies, London, suggests that it may be worth looking more intensively for social bandits in sub-Saharan Africa. His own field-work in Ghana brought knowledge of what 'was and may still be a group of cocoa smugglers who with all the popular acclaim of a Mandrin ran risks along unscheduled roads to get their loads out of Ghana and into Togo'; prices being fixed in one country, free in the other. 'These men were particularly noted for their dash, their conspicuous consumption in an area of comparative poverty. There were songs in Ewe about their brushes with border guards and the police.' They were opposed both to the colonial government and Nkrumah and claimed to support the pan-Ewe party of the Togoland Congress. 'I am perfectly certain that similar stories are to be found all over Africa.' William Pomeroy notes that 'Philippine history, particularly in the nineteenth and twentieth centuries, is crowded with examples of social banditry and of millenarian movements.' His own experience with the Huk guerrillas confirms this impression. Ernst Wangermann draws attention to the Robin Hood characteristics of a German bandit of the late eighteenth century, the Bavarian Hiesl.

Finally, the links between social banditry and social revolution are, so I am told by friends, illustrated by the career of a well-known peasant militant in Bihar, whose varied career as a rebel finally took him into the Indian Communist Party (C.P.I.). He had became so used in his days as a Robin Hood to distribute money taken from landlords to the poor, that it was very difficult to ask him to collect money for the Party, since he tended to share it out rather than pass it to higher organizations. Such are the difficulties of combining the mores of two different kinds of rebellion . . .

I am most grateful to these and other correspondents, as well as to those who put me in the way of further printed sources, some of which have been used in the present revised edition.

*London, August 1971*                                    E. J. H.

# 1

# What is Social Banditry?

We are sad, it is true, but that, is because we have always been
persecuted. The gentry use the pen, we the gun; they are the lords of
the land, we of the mountain.
*An old brigand from Roccamandolfi*[1]

For the law, anyone belonging to a group of men who attack
and rob with violence is a bandit, from those who snatch pay-
rolls at an urban street corner to organized insurgents or
guerrillas who happen not to be officially recognized as such.
Historians and sociologists cannot use so crude a definition. In
this book we shall be dealing only with some kinds of robbers,
namely those who are *not* regarded as simple criminals by public opinion. We shall be dealing essentially with a form of individual or minority rebellion within peasant societies. For the
sake of convenience we shall omit the urban equivalent of the
peasant bandit-rebel, and say little about the more numerous
rural desperadoes who are not peasants by origin or allegiance,
but impoverished gentlemen-robbers. Town and country are
too different as human communities to be easily discussed in
the same terms, and in any case peasant bandits, like most peasants, distrust and hate townsmen. Bandit gentry (most familiar
in the form of the 'robber knights' of late medieval Germany)
are much more mixed up with peasants, but the relationship,
which will be discussed below (pp. 91 and 93) is obscure
and complex.

The point about social bandits is that they are peasant outlaws whom the lord and state regard as criminals, but who remain within peasant society, and are considered by their people
as heroes, as champions, avengers, fighters for justice, perhaps
even leaders of liberation, and in any case as men to be admired, helped and supported. This relation between the ordinary
peasant and the rebel, outlaw and robber is what makes social

banditry interesting and significant. It also distinguishes it from two other kinds of rural crime: from the activities of gangs drawn from the professional 'underworld' or of mere free-booters ('common robbers'), and from communities for whom raiding is part of the normal way of life, such as for instance the Bedouin. In both these cases victims and attackers are strangers and enemies. Underworld robbers and raiders regard the peasants as their prey and know them to be hostile; the robbed in turn regard the attackers as criminals in their sense of the term and not merely by official law. It would be unthinkable for a social bandit to snatch the peasants' (though not the lord's) harvest in his own territory, or perhaps even elsewhere. Those who do therefore lack the peculiar relationship which makes banditry 'social'. Of course in practice such distinctions are often less clear than in theory. A man may be a social bandit on his native mountains, a mere robber on the plains. Nevertheless, analysis requires us to establish the difference.

Social banditry of this kind is one of the most universal social phenomena known to history, and one of the most amazingly uniform. Practically all cases belong to two or three clearly related types, and the variations within these are relatively superficial. What is more, this uniformity is not the consequence of cultural diffusion, but the reflection of similar situations within peasant societies, whether in China, Peru, Sicily, the Ukraine, or Indonesia. Geographically it is found throughout the Americas, Europe, the Islamic world, South and East Asia, and even Australia. Socially it seems to occur in all types of human society which lie between the evolutionary phase of tribal and kinship organization, and modern capitalist and industrial society, but including the phases of disintegrating kinship society and transition to agrarian capitalism.

Tribal or kinship societies are familiar with raiding, but lack the internal stratification which creates the bandit as a figure of social protest and rebellion. However, when such communities, especially those familiar with feuding and raiding such as hunters and pastoralists, develop their own systems of class differentiation, or when they are absorbed into larger economies resting on class conflict, they may supply a disproportionately large number of social bandits, as in Sardinia or the Hungarian Kuncság (the region of the Cumans, one of the last groups of Central Asian pastoral nomads to settle in Europe). In studying such regions it is hard to say at precisely what point the practice of raiding and feuding passes into social banditry, whether in the form of resistance to the rich, to foreign conquerors or oppressors, or to other forces destroying the traditional order of things – all of which may be linked in the minds of bandits, and indeed in reality. However, with luck we may be able to fix the transition chronologically to within one or two generations, e.g. in the Sardinian highlands to the half-century from the 1880s to the 1930s.

At the other end of historic development, modern agrarian systems, both capitalist and post-capitalist, are no longer those of traditional peasant society and cease to produce social bandits. The country which has given the world Robin Hood, the international paradigm of social banditry, has no record of actual social bandits after, say, the early seventeenth century, though public opinion continued to find a more or less unsuitable substitute in the idealization of other kinds of criminal, such as highwaymen. In a broader sense 'modernization', that is to say the combination of economic development, efficient communications and public administration, deprives any kind of banditry, including the social, of the conditions under which it flourishes. In Tsarist Russia, for instance, where brigandage was endemic or epidemic over most of the country until the middle of the eighteenth century, by the end of that century it had disappeared from the immediate neighbourhood of towns, and by the middle of the nineteenth it had, speaking generally, retreated to unsettled and unpacified regions, especially those inhabited by minority peoples. The abolition of serfdom in 1861 marked the end of the long series of government decrees against banditry; the last seems to have been promulgated in 1864.

Otherwise social banditry is universally found, wherever societies are based on agriculture (including pastoral economies), and consist largely of peasants and landless labourers ruled, oppressed and exploited by someone else – lords, towns, governments, lawyers, or even banks. It is found in one or other of its three main forms, each of which will be discussed in a separate chapter: the *noble robber* or Robin Hood, the primitive resistance fighter or guerrilla unit of what I shall call the *haiduks*, and possibly the terror-bringing *avenger*.*

How common such banditry is, cannot be easily discovered. Though the sources give us plenty of examples of bandits, we rarely find estimates for the total numbers active at any one time or quantitive comparisons between the amounts of banditry at different times. Quite clearly its normal amount was modest. The most disturbed part of Colombia at the height of the anarchic civil war of the years after 1948 supported less than forty bands of armed peasants which, reckoning the average robber band at between ten and twenty – a figure surprisingly uniform over the ages and continents – would make between 400 and 800 men for an area of some 23,000 square kilometres, 166 rural settlements and perhaps 6–700,000 rural inhabitants.[†2] Macedonia in the early twentieth century supported a distinctly larger number of bands among its population of, say, one million, but since these were largely financed and organized by various governments, they also represent far more than the spontaneous banditry to be expected in such an area. Even so, it is doubtful whether there were ever more than one or two thousand.[3] If we guess that bandits form no more than 0.1% of the rural population at the outside, we are almost certainly making an ultra-generous estimate.

There are, of course, notable regional variations. They are partly due to geography, partly to technology and administra-

---

* A possible or partial exception might have to be made for the peculiar caste-divided societies of Hindu southern Asia, where social banditry is inhibited by the tendency of robbers, like all other sections of society, to form self-contained castes and communities. However, as we shall see, there are affinities between some kinds of dacoits and social bandits.

† The actual number of armed insurgents during this period was rather larger, but this is not a good measure of even the maximum of banditry in situations other than those of civil war or social breakdown.

tion, partly to social and economic structure. It is a commonplace that brigands flourish in remote and inaccessible areas such as mountains, trackless plains, fenland, forest or estuaries with their labyrinth of creeks and waterways, and are attracted by trade-routes and major highways, where pre-industrial travel is naturally both slow and cumbrous. The construction of good and fast modern roads is often enough to diminish banditry notably. Administrative inefficiency and complication favour it. It is no accident that the Habsburg Empire in the nineteenth century managed its bandit problem more successfully than the ramshackle and effectively decentralized Turkish Empire, or that frontier regions – better still, regions of multiple frontiers like central Germany or the parts of India divided between the British and numerous princely states – were in perpetual difficulties. The ideal situation for robbery is one in which the local authorities are local men, operating in complex local situations, and where a few miles may put the robber beyond the reach or even the knowledge of one set of authorities and into the territory of another, which does not worry about what happens 'abroad'. Lists of areas peculiarly associated with banditry have been drawn up by historians, e.g. for Russia.[4]

Nevertheless, such obvious factors do not account entirely for the marked regional disparities in banditry which are usually found, and which led the Imperial Chinese criminal law, for instance, to establish the distinction between 'brigand areas' (such as the provinces of Szechuan, Honan, Anhwei, Hupeh, Shansi, parts of Kiangsu and Shantung) and others.[5] In the Peruvian departments of Tacna and Moquegua, which were otherwise very suitable, there was no banditry. Why? Because, argues a historian of the subject, 'here there are no landlords, truck-masters or labour contractors, no foremen, no full, absolute or irrevocable lordship over the water supplies'.[6] In other words, because peasant discontent was less. Conversely, an area like Bantam in North Java was a permanent centre of banditry in the nineteenth century, but it was also a permanent centre of rebellion. Only careful regional study can show why banditry was endemic in some parts, weak in other parts of the same country or region. Likewise, only detailed historical study can account for all its 'diachronic' variations. Still, the following generalizations can be made quite safely:

Banditry tended to become epidemic in times of pauperization and economic crisis. The striking increase in Mediterranean brigandage during the late sixteenth century, to which Fernand Braudel has drawn attention, reflected the striking decline in the peasants' condition of life at this period. The Aheriya of Uttar Pradesh (India), always a tribe of hunters, fowlers and thieves, 'did not take to highway robbery till the great famine of 1833'.[7] On a much shorter time-scale, banditry in the Sardinian highlands in the 1960s reached its peak each year when the shepherds' rent fell due. These observations are so platitudinous that they need merely be set down on paper to explain themselves. From the historian's point of view it is more illuminating to distinguish between those crises which signify major historical changes and those which do not, though the distinction will only be grasped slowly and retrospectively by the peasants concerned, if it ever becomes clear to them.

All rural societies of the past were accustomed to periodic dearth – harvest-failure and other natural crises – and to occasional catastrophes, unpredictable in themselves by the villagers, but likely to occur sooner or later, such as wars, conquests, or the breakdown of the administrative system of which they formed a small and remote part. All such catastrophes were likely to multiply banditry of one kind or another. All were likely to pass away, though political breakdowns and wars were also likely to leave behind bands of marauders or other desperadoes for a considerable period, especially if governments were weak or divided. An efficient modern state like France after the Revolution could liquidate the huge epidemic of (nonsocial) brigandage which swept the Rhineland during the 1790s, in a few years. On the other hand the social disruption of the Thirty Years' War left behind in Germany a network of robber bands some of which persisted for at least another century.

Nevertheless, so far as rural society is concerned, things tend to return to normal (including the normally expected amount of social and other banditry) after such traditional disturbances of equilibrium.

The situation is rather different when the events which precipitate an epidemic of banditry are not – to use geographical similes – comparable to earthquakes in Japan or floods in the Low Countries, but reflect long-term changes like the advance of glaciers in an ice-age, or irreversible ones like soil erosion. In such circumstances epidemics of banditry represent more than the simple multiplication of able-bodied men who take what they need by arms rather than starve. They may reflect the disruption of an entire society, the rise of new classes and social structures, the resistance of entire communities or peoples against the destruction of its way of life. Or they may reflect, as in the history of China, the exhaustion of the 'mandate of heaven', the social breakdown which is not due to adventitious forces, but marks the approaching end of a relatively long cycle of history, heralding the fall of one dynasty and the rise of another. Banditry at such times may be the precursor or companion of major social movements such as peasant revolutions. Alternatively, it may itself change by adapting to the new social and political situation, though in doing so it will almost certainly cease to be social banditry. In the typical case of the past two centuries, the transition from a pre-capitalist to a capitalist economy, the social transformation may entirely destroy the kind of agrarian society which gives birth to bandits, the kind of peasantry which nourishes them, and in doing so conclude the history of what is the subject of this book. The nineteenth and twentieth centuries have been the great age of social banditry in many parts of the world, just as the sixteenth to eighteenth probably were in most parts of Europe. Yet it is now largely extinct, except in a few areas.

In Europe it persists on any scale only in the Sardinian highlands, though the aftermath of two bouts of world war and revolution revived it in several regions. Yet in southern Italy, the classic country of the *banditi*, it reached its peak only a century ago, in the great peasant rebellion and guerrilla war of the brigands (1861–5). In Spain, the other classic country of bandits, it was familiar to every nineteenth-century traveller. It still occurs as an expected hazard of tourism in the Edwardian era in Bernard Shaw's *Man and Superman*. However, it was already drawing to an end there. Francisco Ríos ('El Pernales') who operated at this time is the last really legendary brigand of Andalusia. In Greece and the Balkans it is an even more recent memory. In north-east Brazil, where it entered its epidemic phase after 1870, and reached its peak in the first third of the twentieth century, it ended in 1940 and has not revived since. There are certainly regions – perhaps mainly in South and East Asia and one or two parts of Latin America – where old-style social banditry may still be found here and there, and it is not impossible that it may arise in sub-Saharan Africa on a more significant scale than we have had record of in the past. But on the whole social banditry is a phenomenon of the past, though often of the very recent past. The modern world has killed it, though it has substituted its own forms of primitive rebellion and crime.

What part, if any, do bandits play in these transformations of society? As individuals, they are not so much political or social rebels, let alone revolutionaries, as peasants who refuse to submit, and in doing so stand out from their fellows, or even more simply, men who find themselves excluded from the usual career of their kind, and therefore forced into outlawry and 'crime'. *En masse*, they are little more than symptoms of crisis and tension in their society – of famine, pestilence, war or anything else that disrupts it. Banditry itself is therefore not a programme for peasant society but a form of self-help to escape it in particular circumstances. Bandits, except for their willingness or capacity to refuse individual submission, have no ideas other than those of the peasantry (or the section of the peasantry) of which they form a part. They are activists and not ideologists or prophets from whom novel visions or plans of social and political organization are to be expected. They

1. The death in 1818 of Gaetano Meomartino ('Vardarelli') of
Apulia, a revolutionary brigand who joined the Carbonari
c. 1816–17.

are leaders, in so far as tough and self-reliant men often with
strong personalities and military talents are likely to play such
a role; but even then their function is to hack out the way and
not to discover it. Several of the brigand chiefs of southern
Italy in the 1860s, such as Crocco and Ninco Nanco,* showed

* 'Crocco' (Carmine Donatelli), a farm-labourer and cowherd, had joined
the Bourbon army, killed a comrade in a brawl, deserted and lived as an
outlaw for ten years. He joined the liberal insurgents in 1860 in the hope
of an amnesty for his past offences, and subsequently became the most
formidable guerilla chief and leader of men on the Bourbon side. He later
escaped to the Papal States, was handed over to the Italian government and
sentenced to life-imprisonment. In jail, many years later, he wrote an interesting autobiography. 'Ninco Nanco' (Giuseppe Nicola Summa), a landless labourer from Avigliano, had escaped from jail during the Garibaldian
liberation of 1860. As Crocco's lieutenant he also demonstrated brilliant
gifts as a guerilla. Killed in 1864.

gifts of generalship which won the admiration of the officers who fought them, but though the 'years of the brigands' are one of the rare examples of a major peasant rising captained by social banditry, at no stage did the brigand leaders appear to ask their followers to occupy the land, and sometimes they even appeared incapable of conceiving of what would today be called 'agrarian reform'.

Insofar as bandits have a 'programme', it is the defence or restoration of the traditional order of things 'as it should be' (which in traditional societies means as it is believed to have been in some real or mythical past). They right wrongs, they correct and avenge cases of injustice, and in doing so apply a more general criterion of just and fair relations between men in general, and especially between the rich and the poor, the strong and the weak. This is a modest aim, which leaves the rich to exploit the poor (but no more than is traditionally accepted as 'fair'), the strong to oppress the weak (but within the limits of what is equitable, and mindful of their social and moral duties). It demands not that there should be no more lords, or even that lords should not be expected to take their serfs' women, but only that when they did, they should not shirk the obligation to give their bastards an education.* In this sense social bandits are reformers, not revolutionaries.

However, reformist or revolutionary, banditry itself does not constitute a social *movement*. It may be a surrogate for it, as when peasants admire Robin Hoods as their champions, for want of any more positive activity by themselves. It may even be a substitute for it, as when banditry becomes institutionalized among some tough and combative section of the peasantry and actually inhibits the development of other means of struggle. Whether such cases occur has not been clearly established, but there is some evidence that they may. Thus in Peru, the pressure of the peasantry for land reform was (and in 1971 still remained) notably weaker in the departments of Huanuco and Apurimac, where agrarian problems were by no means less acute, but where there was (and is) a very deeply rooted tra-

* I take this example from actual conversations with peasants in Peru.

dition of cattle-rustling and brigandage. However, the question awaits serious investigation, like so many other aspects of banditry.*

Two things may, however, turn this modest, if violent, social objective of bandits – and the peasantry to whom they belong – into genuine revolutionary movements. The first is, when it becomes the symbol, even the spearhead, of resistance by the whole of the traditional order against the forces which disrupt and destroy it. A social revolution is no less revolutionary because it takes place in the name of what the outside world considers 'reaction' against what it considers 'progress'. The bandits of the kingdom of Naples, like its peasantry, who rose against the Jacobins and the foreigners in the name of Pope, King and the Holy Faith were revolutionaries, as Pope and King were not. (As an unusually sophisticated brigand leader in the 1860s told a captive lawyer, who claimed that he too was for the Bourbons: 'You're an educated man and a lawyer: do you really believe we're breaking our bones for Francis II?'†)⁸ They rose not for the *reality* of the Bourbon kingdom – many of them had indeed helped to overthrow it a few months previously under Garibaldi – but for the ideal of the 'good old' society naturally symbolized by the ideal of the 'good old' church and 'good old' king. Bandits in politics tend to be such revolutionary traditionalists.

The second reason why bandits become revolutionaries is inherent in peasant society. Even those who accept exploitation, oppression and subjection as the norm of human life dream of a world without them: a world of equality, brotherhood and freedom, a totally *new* world without evil. Rarely is this more than a dream. Rarely is it more than an apocalyptic expectation, though in many societies the millennial dream persists, the Just Emperor will one day appear, the Queen of the South Seas will

*I am grateful to Dr Mario Vasquez, Enrique Mayer, and various officials of Zone X of Agrarian Reform (Central Peru) for some relevant information.

†Admittedly Cipriano La Gala, an illiterate 'dealer' from Nola, sentenced for robbery with violence in 1855, escaped from jail in 1860, was not typical of the peasant-brigands.

one day land (as in the Javanese version of this submerged hope), and all will be changed and perfect. Yet there are moments when the apocalypse seems imminent; when the entire structure of existing society whose total end the apocalypse symbolizes and predicts, actually looks about to collapse in ruins, and the tiny light of hope turns into the light of a possible sunrise.

At such moments bandits are also swept away, like everyone else. Are they not blood of the people's blood? Are they not men who, in their own limited way, have shown that the wild life in the greenwood can bring liberty, equality and fraternity to those who pay the price of homelessness, danger and almost certain death? (The Brazilian *cangaçeiro* [bandit] bands have been seriously compared by a modern sociologist to 'a sort of brotherhood or lay confraternity', and observers were struck by the unparalleled honesty of personal relations within the bands.)[9] Do they not, consciously or unconsciously, recognize the superiority of the millenial or revolutionary movement to their own activities?

Indeed, nothing is more striking than this subordinate co-existence of banditry with major peasant revolution, of which it thus often serves as a precursor. The area of Andalusia traditionally associated with *bandoleros*, 'noble' or otherwise, became the area traditionally associated with rural anarchism a decade or two after their decline. The *sertão** of north-eastern Brazil, which was the classical home of the *cangaçeiros*, was also that of the *santos*, the rural messianic leaders. Both flourished together, but the saints were greater. The great bandit Lampião, in one of the innumerable ballads which celebrate his exploits,

> Swore to be avenged on all
> Saying in this world I'll respect
> Father Cicero and no one else.[10]

And it was, as we shall see, from Father Cicero, the Messiah of Juazeiro, that public opinion derived Lampião's 'official' cre-

*The back country of north-eastern Brazil beyond the frontiers of concentrated settlement.

dentials. Social banditry and millenarianism – the most primitive forms of reform and revolution – go together historically. And when the great apocalyptic moments come, the brigand bands, their numbers swollen by the time of tribulation and expectation, may insensibly turn into something else. They may, as in Java, merge with the vast mobilizations of villagers who abandon field and house to rove the countryside in exalted hope; they may, as in southern Italy in 1861, find themselves expanding into peasant armies. They may, like Crocco in 1860, cease to be bandits and become soldiers of the revolution.

When banditry thus merges into a large movement, it becomes part of a force which can and does change society. Since the horizons of social bandits are narrow and circumscribed, like those of the peasantry itself, the results of their interventions into history may not be those they expected. They may be the opposite of what they expected. But this does not make banditry any less of a historical force. And in any case, how many of those who made the great social revolutions of the world foresaw the actual results of their endeavours?

# 2

# Who becomes a Bandit?

In Bulgaria only shepherds, cowmen and haiduks are free.
*Panayot Hitov*[1]

Banditry is freedom, but in a peasant society few can be free. Most are shackled by the double chains of lordship and labour, the one reinforcing the other. For what makes peasants the victims of authority and coercion is not so much their economic vulnerability – they are indeed as often as not virtually self-sufficient – as their immobility. Their roots are in the land and the homestead, and there they must stay like trees, or rather like sea-anemones or other sessile aquatic animals which settle down after a phase of youthful mobility. Once a man is married and on his holding, he is tied. The fields must be sown and harvested: even peasant rebellions must stop for the getting in of crops. The fences cannot be left too long unmended. Wife and children anchor a man to an identifiable spot. Only catastrophe, the approach of the millennium, or the grave decision to emigrate, can interrupt the fixed cycle of farming life, but even the emigrant must soon settle down again on some other holding, unless he ceases to be a peasant. The peasant's back is bent socially, because it must generally be bent in physical labour on his field.

This seriously limits the recruitment of bandits. It does not make it impossible for an adult peasant to turn bandit, but nevertheless it is very difficult, all the more so as the annual cycle of robbery follows the same rhythm as that of agriculture, being at its height in spring and summer, in recess during the bare and snowy seasons. (However, communities for whom raiding provides a regular part of their income must combine it with agriculture or pastoralism, and hence their banditry occurs during the off-season, as with the tribal *chuars** of

* Agricultural-cum-raiding tribesmen of the jungle districts in Midnapur (Bengal).

Midnapur [Bengal] in the early nineteenth century; or else it is carried out by special raiding parties, who leave behind enough people to carry out the agricultural work.) If we want to understand the social composition of banditry, we must therefore look primarily at the mobile margin of peasant society.

The first and probably the most important source of bandits is in those forms of rural economy or rural environment which have relatively small labour demands, or which are too poor to employ all their able-bodied men; in other words in the rural surplus population. Pastoral economies and areas of mountain and poor soil, which often go together, provide a permanent surplus of this kind, which tends to develop its own institutionalized outlets in traditional societies: seasonal emigration (as from the Alps or the Kabyle mountains in Algeria), the supply of soldiers (as in Switzerland, Albania, Corsica and Nepal), raiding or banditry. 'Minifundism' (i.e. the prevalence of holdings too small to maintain a family) may have the same effect. So, for even more obvious reasons, may landlessness. The rural proletarian, unemployed for a large part of the year, is 'mobilizable' as the peasant is not. Of the 328 'brigands' or rather, rural insurgents and guerrillas) whose cases were up for review in 1863 by the Court of Appeal in Catanzaro (Calabria, Italy), 201 were described as farm-hands or day-labourers, only fifty-one as peasants, four as farmers, twenty-four as artisans.[2] It is obvious that in such environments there are not only plenty of men who can cut loose, at least for a period, from the rural economy, but who *must* look for other sources of income. Nothing is more natural than that some of them should become bandits, or that mountain and pastoral regions in particular should be the classical zones for such outlawry.

Even so, not everyone in such regions is equally likely to become an outlaw. However, there are always groups whose social posititon gives them the necessary freedom of action. The most important of them is the age-group of male youth between puberty and marriage, i.e. before the weight of full family responsibilities has begun to bend men's backs. (I am told that in countries which permit easy unilateral divorce, the time between the casting-off of one wife and remarriage may be another such episode of relative freedom, but, as with the analogous situation of widowers, this can only be so where there are no small children to be looked after, or where kinsfolk can be got to take care of them.) Even in peasant societies, youth is a phase of independence and potential rebellion. Young men, often united in formal or informal age bands, can move from job to job,

2. In Asian deltas and archipelagos there was no clear distinction between bandits and pirates. Note the watching Jack Tar. From *Banditi and Robbers* (1833).

fight and rove. The *szégeny légeny* ('poor lads') of the Hungarian plains were such potential brigands; harmless enough in isolation, though not disinclined to rustle a head of horse or two, but when united in bands of twenty to thirty with their headquarters in some secluded spot, easily passing over into banditry. It has even been argued (by Eberhard) that the basic stock of Chinese banditry consisted essentially of this temporary youthful village dissidence. At all events there is no doubt whatever that the typical bandit was a young man. Two-thirds of the bandits in the Basilicata of the 1860s were under twenty-five years old. Forty-nine out of fifty-nine bandits in Lambayeque (Peru) were bachelors.[3] Diego Corrientes, the classical bandit-legend of Andalusia, died at twenty-four, Janošik, his Slovak equivalent, at twenty-five, Lampião, the great *cangaçeiro* of the Brazilian north-east, started his career between the ages of seventeen and twenty, the real-life Don José of Carmen at the age of eighteen. Writers can be good observers: 'Slim Mehmed', the hero of a Turkish bandit-novel, went into the Taurus mountains as a teenager.

The second most important source of free men are those who, for one reason or another, are not integrated into rural society and are therefore also forced into marginality or outlawry. The bands of *rasboiniki* (bandits) who flourished in the trackless and thinly-populated spaces of old Russia were composed of such marginal men – often migrants making for the open spaces of the south and east, where lordship, serfdom and government had not yet arrived, in search of what was later to become the consciously revolutionary prospect of *Zemlya i Volya* (Land and Freedom). Some of them did not get there at all, and they all had to live while moving along. So the escaped serfs, ruined freemen, runaways from state or seignorial factories, from jail, seminary, army or navy, men with no determined place in society such as priests' sons, formed or joined brigand bands, which might merge with the raiding of former frontier communities of free peasants such as the Cossacks and national or tribal minorities. (For Cossacks, see Chapter 5 below.)

Among such marginals, soldiers, deserters and ex-servicemen played a significant part. There was good reason for the Tsar to conscript his soldiers for life, for what amounted to life, so that their kinsfolk read the funeral service over them as they bade them farewell at the end of the village. Men who come back from afar, masterless and landless, are a danger to the stability of the social hierarchy. Ex-servicemen like deserters are natural material for banditry. Time and again the leaders of the brigands in southern Italy after 1860 are described as 'ex-soldier of the Bourbon army' or 'landless labourer, ex-soldier'. Indeed in some areas this transformation was normal. Why, asked a progressive Bolivian in 1929, do the ex-servicemen who return to their settlements among the Aymara Indians not act as educators and agents of civilization instead of 'turning into loafers and degenerates who become leaders of the bandits of this region'?[4] The question was just, but rhetorical. Ex-servicemen *can* act as leaders, educators and village cadres, and all socially revolutionary régimes use their armies as training schools for this purpose, but who would have really expected this in feudal Bolivia?

Few except returned ex-soldiers are entirely if temporarily outside the village economy, though still part of peasant society (as gypsies, and other *fahrendes Volk* or vagrants normally are not). However, the rural economy provides for a number of jobs which are outside the common routine of labour and the immediate range of social control, whether by the rulers or the public opinion of the ruled. There are, once again, the herdsmen, alone or with others of their kind – a special, sometimes a secret group – on the high pastures during the season of summer pasture, or roving as semi-nomads across the wide plains. There are the armed men and field-guards, whose job is not to labour, the drovers, carters and smugglers, bards and others of the kind. They are not watched, but rather watchers themselves. Indeed as often as not the mountains provide their common world, into which landlords and ploughmen do not enter, and where men do not talk much about what they see and do. Here bandits meet shepherds, and shepherds consider whether to become bandits.

The sources of potential bandits we have considered so far are all collectives, that is to say social categories of men any one of whom is more likely to become a bandit than any one of the members of some other category. They are clearly very important. For instance, they enable us to make brief, approximate, but not fundamentally misleading generalizations such as: 'The characteristic bandit unit in a highland area is likely to consist of young herdsmen, landless labourers and ex-soldiers and unlikely to contain married men with children or artisans.' Such formulae do not exhaust the question, but they do cover a surprisingly large part of the field. For instance, of the south Italian band-leaders in the 1860s, those for whom we have occupational descriptions include twenty-eight 'shepherds', 'cow-herds', 'ex-servicemen', 'landless labourers' and 'field guards' (or combinations of these occupations) and only five others.[5] Nevertheless, there is another category of potential bandits, in some ways the most important, membership of which is, as it were, individual and voluntary, though it may well overlap with the others. This consists of the men who are unwilling to accept the meek and passive social role of the subject peasant; the stiffnecked and recalcitrant, the individual rebels. They are, in the classic familiar peasant phrase, the 'men who make themselves respected'.

There may not be many of them in ordinary peasant society, but there are always some. These are the men who, when faced with some act of injustice or persecution, do not yield meekly to force or social superiority, but take the path of resistance and outlawry. For we must remember that, if resistance to such acts of oppression is the characteristic start of a 'noble' robber's career, for every resister there must be scores who accept injustice. A Pancho Villa who defends the honour of a raped sister is the exception in societies in which lords and their henchmen do as they will with peasant girls. These are the men who establish their right to be respected against all comers, including other peasants, by standing up and fighting – and in so doing automatically usurp the social role of their 'betters' who, as in the classic medieval ranking system, have the monopoly of fighting. They may be the toughs, who advertise their toughness by their swagger, their carrying of arms, sticks or clubs, even when peasants are not supposed to go armed, by the casual and rakish costume and manner which symbolize toughness. The 'bare-stick' of the old Chinese village (commonly translated as 'village bully' by old China hands) wore his pig-

tail loose, its end coiled round head and neck; his shoes de-
liberately down-at-heel; his leggings open to allow the expensive
lining to show. He was often said to provoke the magistrate
'out of sheer bravado'.[6] The *vaqueiro* (or cowpuncher) outfit of
the Mexican herd-riders which has become the classic cowboy
costume of the Westerns, and the more or less equivalent styles
of *gauchos* and *llaneros* on the South-American plains, *bétyars**
on the Hungarian *puszta*, *majos* and *flamencos†* in Spain, are
examples of similar symbols of unsubmissiveness in the western
world. Such symbolism reached perhaps its most elaborate expression in the gold- and steel-festooned costume of the Balkan
*haiduk* or *klepht*. For, as in all traditional and slow-changing
societies, even the loose group of the non-conformist poor becomes formalized and recognized by outward signs. The
rural tough's outfit is a code which reads: 'This man is not
tame.'

Those 'who make themselves respected' do not automatically
become bandits, or at least not social bandits. They may fight
their way out of the peasant's lot by becoming village guards,
lord's retainers or soldiers (which means official bandits of
various kinds). They may look after themselves and become a
strong-arm rural bourgeoisie, like the *Mafiosi* of Sicily. They
may also become the kind of outlaws about whom men sing
ballads: champions, heroes and avengers. Theirs is an individual rebellion, which is socially and politically undetermined,
and which under normal – i.e. non-revolutionary – conditions is
not a vanguard of mass revolt, but rather the product and
counterpart of the general passivity of the poor. They are the
exception which proves the rule.

These categories more or less exhause the sources which
supply peasant bandits. However, we must briefly consider two
other reservoirs of rural violence and robbery, which are some-

* *Gauchos, llaneros, bétyars*. Various names for cowboys. *Bétyar* is
technically a kind of irregularly employed labourer.

† *Majo* and *flamenco* are descriptions of a style of dress and behaviour
summarized in an eighteenth-century Spanish dictionary as 'the man who
affects valour and panache in word and action'.

times rightly, but in most cases quite mistakenly, confused with peasant banditry: 'robber barons' and criminals.

It stands to reason that impoverished country gentlemen provide an endless supply of toughs. Arms are their privilege, fighting their vocation and the basis of their system of values. A good deal of this violence is institutionalized in such pursuits as hunting, the defence of personal and family 'honour' by duels and vengeance and suchlike, or channelled by careful governments into politically useful or at least harmless outlets such as military service and colonial adventure. Dumas's Musketeers, the products of that well-known nursery of impecunious gentlemen, Gascony, were plainly little more than officially licensed bullies with a pedigree, analogous to the peasant or shepherd roughnecks hired as guards by Italian or Iberian latifundists. So were many of the Spanish *conquistadores*. There are, however, situations, in which such pauper squires become actual outlaws and robbers (see Chapter 6 below). We may guess that the outlaw gentlemen is most likely to enter the realm of popular myth and ballad (a) when he can form part of a general movement of resistance by some archaic society against outsiders or foreign conquest; or (b) when there is only a feeble tradition of active peasant rebellion against seignorial injustice. He is least likely to enter it where the element of class struggle is most pronounced, though of course in countries with a high proportion of 'gentlemen', such as Poland, Hungary and Spain, where they formed perhaps ten per cent of the total population, they provided a large public for ballads and romances about themselves.*

There is an even sharper division between peasant bandits

*The classification of bandit songs and ballads is complicated by two factors. First, the tendency of 'official' culture to upgrade them socially as the price of assimilating them, i.e. to turn Robin Hood into a wronged Earl of Huntingdon; second the tendency of all free men in feudal types of rural society to assimilate their own status to the only familiar model of 'freedom', i.e. the status of 'nobility'. Possibly the latter accounts for the belief that unquestioned Hungarian peasant bandits of the nineteenth century, like Sandor Rósza and Sóbry Jószi, were noblemen of old family; possibly the former.

and the criminal underworld of urban or vagrant elements, which existed in the interstices of rural society but clearly did not belong to it. In traditional societies criminals are almost by definition outsiders, who form their own separate society, if not actually an anti-society of the 'bent' which mirrors that of the 'straight'. They normally speak their own special language (argot, cant, *caló, Rotwelsch*). Their associations are with other outcast occupations or communities, like the gypsies, who supplied so much of the argot of the French and Spanish underworld, the Jews who provided even more vocabulary to the German. (The bulk of peasant bandits speak no kind of argot, but simply a version of the local peasant dialect.) They are non-conformists, or rather anti-conformists in practice and by ideology; on the devil's side rather than God's,*[7] or if religious, then on the side of heresy against orthodoxy. In the seventeenth century Christian villains in Germany petitioned to join the religious services of the Jews in jail, and there is quite strong evidence (echoed in Schiller's play *The Robbers*) that eighteenth-century German bands provided a refuge for libertinist or antinomian sectarians, such as survivors of central-German anabaptism.[8] Peasant bandits are in no sense heterodox, but share the value-system of ordinary peasants, including their piety, and their suspicion of out-groups. (Thus, except in the Balkans, most central and east European social bandits were anti-semitic.)

Where bands of criminal robbers roam the countryside, as in parts of central Europe in the seventeenth and eighteenth centuries, or in India, they can therefore normally be distinguished from social bandits both by their composition and their mode of operation. They are likely to consist of members of 'criminal tribes and castes', or individuals from outcast groups. Thus the Crefeld and Neuss gang of the 1790s, like Keil's gang, was composed largely of knife-grinders, while in Hesse-Waldeck there was a gang composed mainly of rag-and-bone men. About

---

*'A robber who had not made a pact with the devil was unthinkable, especially in the sixteenth century, and until recent times the devil has occupied the first place in the dogmatic system of the robbers.'

half of the Salembier gang which made the Pas-de-Calais unsafe in the same period were hawkers, dealers in second-hand goods, fairground people and the like. The formidable Low Countries gang, with most of its various sub-units, was largely Jewish. And so on. Criminal vocations were often hereditary: the Bavarian woman robber Schattinger had a family tradition of two hundred years to look back upon, and more than twenty of her kin, including her father and sister, were in jail or had been executed.[9] It is not surprising that they did not seek the sympathy of the peasantry, since they, like all the 'straight' people, were their enemies, oppressors and victims. Criminal bands thus lacked the local roots of social bandits, but at the same time they were not confined by the limits of the territory beyond which social bandits could rarely venture in safety. They formed part of large, if loose networks of an underworld which might stretch over half a continent, and would certainly extend into the cities which were *terra incognita* for peasant bandits who feared and hated them. For vagrants, nomads, criminals and their like, the kind of area within which most social bandits lived out their lives, was merely a location for so many markets or fairs a year, a place for occasional raids, or at most (for instance if strategically placed near several frontiers) a suitable headquarters for wider operations.

Nevertheless, criminal robbers cannot be simply excluded from the study of social banditry. In the first place, where for one reason or another social banditry did not flourish or had died out, suitable criminal robbers might well be idealized and given the attributes of Robin Hood, especially when they concentrated on holding up merchants, rich travellers, and others who enjoyed no great sympathy among the poor. Thus in eighteenth-century France, England and Germany celebrated underworld characters like Dick Turpin, Cartouche and Schinderhannes substituted for the genuine Robin Hoods who had disappeared from these countries by that time.*

* Dick Turpin 1705–39; Cartouche 1693–1721; 'Schinderhannes' (Johannes Pueckler) 1783–1803. The other French bandit–hero of the eighteenth century, Robert Mandrin, 1724–55 was a somewhat less

In the second place, involuntary outcasts from the peasantry, such as the ex-soldiers, deserters and marauders who abounded in periods of disorder, war or its aftermath, provided a link between social and anti-social banditry. Such men would have fitted easily into social bands, but attached themselves with equal ease to the others, bringing to them some of the values and assumptions of their native environment. In the third place, old-established and permanent pre-industrial empires had long developed a double underworld: not only that of the outcast, but also that of unofficial mutual defence and opposition, as typified by the great and long-lasting secret societies of Imperial China or Vietnam, or perhaps by bodies like the Sicilian Mafia. Such unofficial political systems and networks, which are still very poorly understood and known, might reach out to all who were outside and against the official structure of power, including both social bandits and the outsider groups. They might, for instance, provide both with the alliances and resources which, under certain circumstances, turned banditry into a nucleus of effective political rebellion.

However, though in practice social banditry cannot always be clearly separated from other kinds of banditry, this does not affect the fundamental analysis of the social bandit as a special type of peasant protest and rebellion. This is what forms the main subject of the present book.

---

unsuitable candidate for idealization. He was a professional smuggler from the Franco–Swiss border region, a trade never considered criminal by anybody except governments; and he was engaged on a campaign of vengeance.

# 3
# The Noble Robber

On that night the moon was dim and the light of the stars filled the sky.
They had gone but a little more than three miles when they saw the
crowd of carts and upon the banners over them was written clearly 'The
grain of the righteous and Loyal Robbers' Lair'.

*The Shui Hu Chuan*[1]

WICKED: A man who kills Christians without a deep reason.
*From a word association test given to the famous Calabrian bandit Musolino.*[2]

Robin Hood, the noble robber, is the most famous and universally popular type of bandit, the most common hero of
ballad and song in theory, though scarcely in practice. There is
no mystery in this disproportion between legend and fact, any
more than there is in the divergence between the realities of
medieval knighthood and the dream of chivalry. Robin Hood
is what all peasant bandits should be, but in the nature of
things, few of them have the idealism, the unselfishness, or the
social consciousness to live up to their role, and perhaps few
can afford to. Still, the ones who do – and genuine Robin Hoods
have been known – enjoy the veneration due to heroes, even to
saints. Diego Corrientes (1757–81), the noble robber of Andalusia, was, according to popular opinion, similar to Christ: he
was betrayed, delivered to Seville on a Sunday, tried on a Fri-
day in March, and yet had killed nobody.[3] The real Juro
Janošik (1688–1713) was, like most social bandits, a provincial
robber in some lost corner of the Carpathians whose existence
would barely attract the attention of the authorities in the capital. But literally hundreds of songs about him survive to the
present day. On the other hand, such is the need for heroes and
champions, that if there are no real ones, unsuitable candidates
are pressed into service. In real life most Robin Hoods were far
from noble.

It is therefore as well to begin with the 'image' of the noble robber, which defines both his social role and his relationship

3. Three heroes of the Robin Hood cycle in the seventeenth-century Roxburghe Ballads. Note the longbow, a commoner's weapon.

with the common peasants. His role is that of the champion, the righter of wrongs, the bringer of justice and social equity. His relation with the peasants is that of total solidarity and identity. The 'image' reflects both. It may be summarized in nine points.

First, the noble robber begins his career of outlawry not by crime, but as the victim of injustice, or through being persecuted by the authorities for some act which they, but not the custom of his people, consider as criminal.

Second, he 'rights wrongs'.

Third, he 'takes from the rich to give to the poor'.

Fourth, he 'never kills but in self-defence or just revenge'.

Fifth, if he survives, he returns to his people as an honourable citizen and member of the community. Indeed, he never actually leaves the community.

Sixth, he is admired, helped and supported by his people.

Seventh, he dies invariably and only through treason, since no decent member of the community would help the authorities against him.

Eighth, he is – at least in theory – invisible and invulnerable.

Ninth, he is not the enemy of the king or emperor, who is the fount of justice, but only of the local gentry, clergy or other oppressors.

Indeed, the facts largely confirm the image, insofar as it represents reality and not wish-fulfilment. Social bandits do, in the great majority of recorded cases, begin their career with some non-criminal dispute, affair of honour or as victims of what they and their neighbours feel to be injustice (which may be no more than the automatic consequence of a dispute between one of the poor and one of the rich and influential). Angelo Duca or 'Angiolillo' (1760–84), a Neapolitan bandit of the eighteenth century, became an outlaw over some dispute about strayed cattle with a field-guard of the Duke of Martina; Pancho Villa in Mexico revenging the honour of his sister against a landowner; Labarêda, like practically all Brazilian *cangaçeiros*, over an affair of family honour; Giuliano as a young smuggler – as honourable a trade as any in the mountains – for resisting a revenue man whom he was too poor to bribe. And so on. And indeed it is essential for the Robin Hood to start in this way, for if he were to be a *real* criminal, by the moral standards of his community, how could he enjoy its unqualified support?

To begin as the victim of injustice is to be imbued with the need to right at least one wrong: the bandit's own. It is natural enough that real bandits often demonstrate that 'savage spirit of justice' which observers noted in José Maria 'El Tempranillo' (the original Don José of *Carmen*) who operated in the Andalusian hills. In the legend this righting of wrongs often takes the form of a literal transfer of wealth. Jesse James (1847–82) is supposed to have lent a poor widow $800 to meet her debt to a banker, then to have held up the banker and taken the money back; an improbable story from all we know of the James brothers.* In extreme cases, as in Schiller's drama *The Robbers*, the noble bandit offers his own life in exchange for justice for some poor man. Just so in real life (or was it in contemporary legend?) Zelim Khan, the Robin Hood of early twentieth-century Daghestan, cornered in a mountain cave, sent word through a shepherd to the opposing commander:

'Go tell the chief of the district that I shall give myself up to him when he shows me a telegram on a paper from the Tsar saying he will withdraw all fines imposed on innocents; and furthermore that a free pardon will be issued to all detained and exiled on account of me. But if not, then tell Prince Karavlov that this very night, before midnight, I shall escape from this cave, in spite of everything and everyone. Till then I await his answer.'

In practice rough justice is more likely to take the form of vengeance and retribution, Zelim Khan, to quote him again, wrote to a Moslem officer, a certain Donugayev:

'Take note that I kill the representatives of authority because they have illegally exiled my poor people to Siberia. When Col. Popov was head of Grozniy district there was an uprising, and the representatives of authority and the army felt they had to assert themselves by massacring several poor unfortunates. When I heard this I assembled my band and looted a train at Kadi-Yurt. There I killed Russians for vengeance.'[4]

Whatever the actual practice, there is no doubt that the bandit is considered an agent of justice, indeed a restorer of morality, and often considers himself as such.

Whether he takes from the rich to give to the poor is a much-debated question, though it is evident that he cannot afford to take from the local poor if he is to retain their support against the authorities. There is no question that 'noble' bandits have the reputation of redistributing wealth. 'Banditry in Lambayeque has always been distinguished', writes Colonel of the

*The identical story is told of Mate Cosido, the leading social bandit of the Argentine Chaco in the 1930s.

*Guardia Civil* Victor Zapata, 'by its gallantry, valour, finesse and the disinterestedness of the brigands. Neither bloodthirsty nor cruel, these used, in most cases, to distribute their booty among the poor and hungry, thus showing that they were not lost to feelings of charity and had not hardened their hearts.'[5] The distinction between bandits who have this reputation and those who have not is very clear in the mind of the local population, including (as the above quotation suggests) the police itself. There is also no question that some bandits do sometimes give to the poor, whether in the form of individual beneficence or indiscriminate largesse. Pancho Villa distributed the proceeds of his first major coup as follows: five thousand pesos to his mother, four thousand to the families of relatives and

I bought a tailor's shop for a man named Antonio Retana who had very poor eyesight and a large and needy family. I hired a man to run it and gave him the same amount of money. And so it went on. By the end of eight or ten months all that I had left of the 50,000 pesos went to help people in need.[6]

On the other hand Luis Pardo, the Robin Hood of Peruvian banditry (1874–1909) seems to have preferred scattering handfuls of silver among the crowds at fiestas, as in his native town of Chiquian, or 'sheets, soap, biscuits, tins of food, candles etc.', bought in the local shops, as in Llaclla.[7] No doubt, many bandits may have gained their reputation for generosity simply through paying generously for the services, food and shelter of the local population. This, at least, is the view of Esteban Montejo, an unromantic ancient Cuban disinclined to sentimentalize the bandits of his youth.[8] Still, even he admits that 'when they robbed a good big sum, they went and shared it out'. Naturally in pre-industrial societies liberality and charity are a moral obligation for the 'good' man of power and wealth. Sometimes, as among the dacoits of India, they are formally institutionalized. The Badhaks – most famous of robber communities in northern India – set aside 4,500 rupees out of a haul of 40,000 for sacrifice to the gods and charity. The Minas were celebrated for their charity.[9] Conversely, there are no ballads about the rather insolvent bandits of Piura, a fact which the student of Peruvian banditry explains by their being too poor to distribute their loot to the other poor. In other words, taking from the rich and giving to the poor is a familiar and established custom, or at least an ideal moral obligation, whether in the green wood of Sherwood Forest or in the American south-west of Billy the Kid who, the story goes, 'was good to Mexicans. He was like Robin Hood; he'd steal from white people and give it to the Mexicans, so they thought he was all right.'[10]

Moderation in the use of violence is an equally important part of the Robin Hood image. 'He robs the rich, helps the poor and kills nobody', ran the phrase about Diego Corrientes of Andalusia. Ch'ao Kai, one of the bandit leaders in the classic Chinese Water Margin novel, asks after a raid: 'Was no man killed?', and when told that nobody was hurt 'Ch'ao Kai, hearing this, was mightily pleased and said "From this day on we are not to injure people".'[11] Melnikov, an ex-Cossack operating near Orenburg 'killed but rarely'. The Catalan brigands of the sixteenth and seventeenth centuries, at least in the ballads, must kill only in defence of their honour; even Jesse James and Billy the Kid were required by their legend to kill only in self-defence or for other just causes. This abstention from wanton violence is all the more astonishing, since the sort of environment in which bandits operate is often one in which all men go armed, where killing is normal, and where in any case the safest maxim is to shoot first and ask questions later. In any case it is hard to suppose that any of their contemporaries who knew them seriously believed that the James brothers or Billy the Kid thought twice about killing anyone in their way.

Whether any real bandit was ever in a position to live consistently up to this moral requirement of his status is therefore very doubtful. Whether he was ever really expected to, is also by no means clear; for though the moral imperatives of a peasant society are sharp and defined, men used to poverty and helplessness usually make an equally sharp distinction between those commandments which are genuinely binding in virtually all circumstances – e.g. not talking to the police – and those which, from necessity or destitution, can be dispensed with.* And yet, the very familiarity of killing and violence makes men extremely sensitive to moral distinctions which escape more pacific societies. There is just or legitimate killing and unjust, unnecessary and wanton murder; there are honourable and shameful acts. This distinction applies both to the judgement of those who are the potential victims of armed violence, the peaceable submissive peasantry, and to the fighters themselves, whose code may well be a rough chivalry, which frowns on the killing of the helpless, and even on the 'unfair' attacks on recognized and open adversaries such as the *local* police, with whom the bandit may be linked in mutual respect. (The rules which apply to outsiders are rather different.)† Whatever the definition of 'just' killing, the 'noble bandit' must at least seek to remain within it, and it is probable that the true social bandit does. We shall have occasion later to consider the type of bandit to whom this limitation does not apply.

Since the social bandit is not a criminal, he has no difficulty in rejoining his community as a respected member when he ceases to be an outlaw.‡ The documents are unanimous on this point. Indeed, he may never actually leave it. In most cases he is

---

*Juan Martinez Alier has made this point with great force on the basis of a series of interviews with rural labourers in Andalusia in 1964–5.[12]

† Yashar Kemal's novel *Mehmed My Hawk* gives some good illustrations of this relationship. The hero warns the local sergeant, who spends most of his time pursuing bandits, to take cover when he happens to surprise him. Conversely, the sergeant has cornered Mehmed in a mountain cave, with his wife, new-born baby and another woman. To save them Mehmed offers to give himself up. The sergeant advances to take his surrender, but one of the women taunts him: 'You think you have captured him in fair fight, but you have only won because he cannot let the child die.' And the sergeant cannot bring himself to take the celebrated outlaw in, for there would be no glory in such a victory: he lets him escape.

‡ Luis Borrego, companion to the famous 'El Tempranillo', even managed subsequently to become the mayor of the township of Benameji; admittedly a settlement which has traditionally shown no bias against bandits.[13]

likely to operate within the territory of his village or kinsfolk, being maintained by them as a matter of family duty as well as common sense, for if they did not feed him, would he not be obliged to become a common robber? The point is made with equal conviction by a Habsburg student of Bosnia and a Corsican official of the French Republic: 'Better to feed them than that they should steal.'[14] In remote and inaccessible areas, where the agents of authority enter only on occasional forays, the bandit may actually live in the village, unless word should come that the police are on the way; thus in the wilds of Calabria or Sicily. Indeed in the real back country, where law and government leave only the faintest trace, the bandit may be not only tolerated and protected, but a leading member of the community, as often in the Balkans.

Consider the case of a certain Kota Christov of Roulia, in the depth of late nineteenth-century Macedonia. He was the most feared bandleader of the region, but at the same time the recognized leading citizen of his village, its headman, shop-keeper, innkeeper and jack of all trades. On behalf of his village he resisted the local (mostly Albanian) landowners and defied the Turkish officials who came to requisition food for soldiers and gendarmes, with whom he always passed the time of day and who never attempted to disturb him. A devout Christian, he knelt before the shrine at the Byzantine monastery of the Holy Trinity after every one of his exploits, and deplored the wanton killing of Christians, though not, we may suppose, Albanians of any religion.* Kota was unquestionably not a simple robber, and though extremely shaky by modern ideological standards – he fought first for the Turks, then for the Internal Macedonian Revolutionary Organization, later still for the Greeks – a systematic defender of 'his' people's rights against injustice and oppression. Moreover, he seems to have made a clear distinction between permissible and impermissible attacks, which may reflect either a sense of justice or of local politics; at all events he expelled two of his band for killing a certain Abdin Bey,

* Curiously enough, he became a hero among the Albanians, who have a song about him.[15]

though he had himself dispatched a number of other local tyrants. The only reason why such a man cannot be simply classified as a social bandit is that in the political conditions of Turkish Macedonia, he was hardly an outlaw at all, at least for most of the time. Where the bonds of government and lordship were loose, Robin Hood was a recognized community leader.

It is only natural that the people's champion should not only be, by local standards, honest and respectable, but entirely admirable. As we have seen, the Robin Hood 'image' insists on morally positive actions such as robbing the rich and not killing too much, but more than this, it insists on the standard attributes of the morally approved citizen. Peasant societies make very clear distinctions between the social bandits who deserve, or are believed to deserve, such approval, and those who, though sometimes celebrated, feared and even admired, do not. Several languages indeed have separate words for these different types of robbers. There are plenty of ballads which end with the famous robber confessing his sins on his deathbed, or

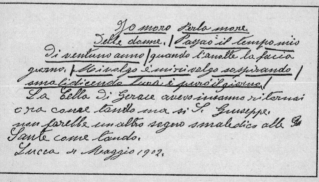

4. Autograph of Musolino. The famous Calabrian brigand recalls a dream in jail and writes a prose close to poetry.

atoning for his awful deeds, like the haiduk *voivode* Indje, whom the earth vomited forth three times before he found rest in his grave when a dead dog was placed in it with him.[16] That is not the fate of the noble robber, for he has committed no sin. On the contrary, the people pray for his safety, like the women of San Stefano in Aspromonte (Calabria) for the great Musolino.[17]

> Musolino is innocent.
> They have condemned him unjustly;
> Oh Madonna, oh Saint Joseph,
> Let him always be under your protection ...
> Oh Jesus, oh my Madonna,
> Keep him from all harm
> Now and forever, so let it be.

For the noble bandit is *good*. To take a case where reality and image are in some conflict, Jesse James was supposed never to have robbed preachers, widows, orphans or ex-Confederates. What is more, he was supposed to have been a devout Baptist who taught in a church singing school. The dirt-farmers of Missouri could hardly go further in establishing his moral bona fides.

A man of this sort would naturally be helped by one and all, and since nobody would help the law against him, and he would be virtually beyond discovery by clumsy soldiers and gendarmes in the country he knew so well, only treason could lead to his capture. As the Spanish ballad has it:

> Two thousand escudos of silver
> They will give for his head alone.
> Many would win the prize,
> But nobody can succeed,
> Only a comrade could.[18]

In practice as well as in theory bandits perish by treason, though the police may claim the credit, as with Giuliano. (There is even a Corsican proverb about this: 'Killed after death, like a bandit by the police'.) The ballads and tales are full of these execrated traitors, from the time of Robin Hood himself to the twentieth century: Robert Ford, who betrayed Jesse James, Pat Garrett, the Judas of Billy the Kid, or Jim Murphy who gave away Sam Bass:

> Oh what a scorching Jim will get
> When Gabriel blows his horn.

But so are the documented stories of the death of bandits: Oleksa Dovbuš, the Carpathian bandit of the eighteenth century, did not die through the betrayal of his mistress Eržika, as the songs have it, but he was killed by the peasant Stepan Dzvinka, whom he had aided, shot in the back. Salvatore Giuliano was betrayed, and so were Angiolillo and Diego Corrientes. For how else could such men die?

Were they not invisible and invulnerable? 'People's bandits' are always believed to be, probably unlike other desperadoes, and the belief reflects their identification with the peasantry. They are always going about the countryside in impenetrable disguises, or in the dress of an ordinary man, unrecognized by the forces of authority until they reveal themselves. For since nobody will give them away and they are indistinguishable from common men, they are *as good as* invisible. The anecdotes merely give a symbolic expression to this relationship. Their invulnerability seems to be a somewhat more complex phenomenon. To some extent it also reflects the security which bandits have among their people and on their own ground. To some extent it expresses the wish that the people's champion cannot be defeated, the same sort of wish that produces the perennial myths of the good king – and the good bandit – who has not really died, but will come back one day to restore justice. Refusal to believe in a robber's death is a certain criterion of his 'nobility'. Thus Sergeant Romano was not really killed, but may still be seen roaming the countryside secretly and in solitude; Pernales (one of several Andalusian bandits about whom such stories are told) 'really' got away to Mexico; Jesse James to California. For the bandit's defeat and death is the defeat of his people; and what is worse, of hope. Men can live without justice, and generally must, but they cannot live without hope.

However, the bandit's invulnerability is not only symbolic. It is almost invariably due to magic, which reflects the beneficent interest of the divinities in his affairs. South Italian brigands had amulets blessed by Pope or King, and regarded themselves as being under the protection of the virgin; those of southern Peru appealed to Our Lady of Luren, those of north-eastern

Brazil to the local holy men. In certain societies with strongly institutionalized brigandage, such as south and south-east Asia, the magical element is even more highly developed and its significance is perhaps clearer. Thus the traditional Javanese 'rampok' band is essentially a 'group formation of a magical–mystical nature', and its members are united, in addition to other bonds, by the *ilmoe* (elmu), a magical charm which may consist of a word, an amulet, an adage, but sometimes simply personal conviction, and which is in turn acquired by spiritual exercises, meditation and the like, by gift or purchase, or which comes to a man at birth, designating him for his vocation. It is this which makes robbers invisible and invulnerable, paralyses their victims or sends them to sleep, and allows them to fix, by divination, the place, day and hour of their exploits – but also forbids them to vary the plan once it has been divinely determined. The interesting point about this Indonesian bandit magic is that it can under certain circumstances be generalized. At moments of high millennial excitement, when the masses themselves rise in expectation, they also believe themselves to be magically invulnerable. Magic therefore may express the spiritual legitimacy of the bandit's action, the function of leadership in the band, the compelling force of the cause. But perhaps it may also be seen as a sort of double insurance policy: one which supplements human skill,* but which also explains human failure. For if the omens have been read wrongly, or one or other of the magical conditions have not been fulfilled, the defeat of the invulnerable hero does not imply the defeat of the ideal which he represents. And, alas, the poor and weak know that their champions and defenders are not really in-

---

*Indonesian bandit leaders have strong magic only if they also prove their fitness to lead by success in action; the Aheriya dacoits of UP took omens before their robberies, but very brave *jemadars* (leaders) might not bother to.[19] A song about Lampião puts the matter very clearly, as usual. The great bandit was treated by master Macumba, a *feiticeiro* (witchdoctor or magician) with the African magic which, as all know, is the strongest, to make him invulnerable to gun and knife; but the wizard also told him, in case of need, to appeal to 'Saint Legs, St Vigilant, St Rifle, St Suspicious, St Lookout', etc.

vulnerable. They may always rise again – but they will also be defeated and killed.

Finally, since the noble robber is just, he cannot be in real conflict with the fount of justice, whether divine or human. There are a number of versions of the story of conflict and reconciliation between bandit and king. The Robin Hood cycle alone contains several. The king, on the advice of evil counsellors such as the Sheriff of Nottingham, pursues the noble outlaw. They fight, but the king cannot vanquish him. They meet and the ruler, who naturally recognizes the outlaw's virtue, allows him to continue his good work, or even takes him into his own service.* The symbolic meaning of these anecdotes is clear. It is less evident that, if not actually true, they may still rest on experiences which make them plausible enough to people in the kind of environments in which banditry abounds. Where the state is remote, ineffective and weak, it will indeed be tempted to come to terms with any local power-group it cannot defeat. If robbers are successful enough, they have to be conciliated just like any other centre of armed force. Every person who lives in times when banditry has got out of hand knows that local officials have to establish a working relationship with robber chiefs, just as every citizen of New York knows that the police has such relationships with the 'mobs' (see below p. 88). It is neither incredible nor unprecedented that famous bandits should be pardoned and given official posts by the king, e.g. El Tempranillo (Don José) in Andalusia. Nor is it incredible that Robin Hoods, whose ideology is precisely the same as that of the surrounding peasantry, should think of themselves as 'loyal and righteous'. The only difficulty is that the closer a bandit comes to the people's ideal of a 'noble robber', i.e. to being the socially conscious champion of the rights of the poor, the less likely is it that the authorities will open their arms to him. They are much more apt to treat him as a social revolutionary and hunt him down.

This should normally take them not more than two or three

* Historians have even tried to authenticate the existence of Robin Hood by searching the royal accounts for wages paid to an R. Hood by the king.

# Robin Hoods Chase.

### OR,

A Merry Progreſs between *Robin Hood* and King *Henry*:
Shewing how *Robin Hood* led the King his Chaſe, from *London* to *London*, and when he had
ſpoken with the Queen, he returned to merry *Sherewood*.
To the Tune of, *Robin Hood and the beggar.*

Come you gallants all, to you I do call
  with hey down, down, an a down,
that now is within this place,
For a ſong I will ſing, of Henry the King,
  how he did Robin Hood chaſe.

Queen Katherine ſhe a match did make,
  with hey, &c.
  as plainly doth appear,
For three hundred tun of good red Wine,
  and three hundred tun of beer.

But yet her Archers ſhe had to ſeek,
  with hey, &c.
with their Bows and Arrows ſo good,
But her mind was bent, with a good intent
  to ſend for bold Robin Hood.

And when bold Robin hood he came there,
  with hey, &c.
  Queen Katherine ſhe did ſay,
Thou art welcome Locksly ſaid the Quéen
  and all thy yeomen gay.

For a match of ſhooting I have made,
  with hey, &c.
  and thou on my part muſt be:
Robin,
If I miſs the mark, be it light or dark,
  even hanged I will be,
But when the Game it come to be play'd
  with hey, &c.

bold Robin then drew nigh,      (ſée it
  with his Mantle of green, moſt brave to be
  ye let his Arrows flye.

And when the Game it ended was,
  with hey, &c.
  bold Robin wan it with a grace,
Then after the King was angry with him
  and thought he would him chaſe.

What though his pardon granted was,
  with hey down, &c.
Yet after the King was try'd at him,
  when he was gone his way.

Soon after the King from the Court did
  with hey, &c.      (hye,
  in a furious angry mood,
And did often enquire, both far and near,
  after bold Robin Hood.

And when the King to Nottingham came
  with hey, &c.
  bold Robin was in the ſwood :
O come now ſaid he, and let me ſee,
  who can find me bold Robin Hood.

But when that Robin Hood he did hear,
  with hey down, down an a down,
  the King had him in chaſe :
Then ſaid little John, 'tis time to be gone
  and go to ſome other place.

5. The king pursues Robin Hood and then makes his peace with
him: a familiar theme in the myth of the 'noble' robber.

years, the average span of a Robin Hood's career, unless he operates in some very remote region and/or enjoys a very great deal of political protection.* For if the authorities really bring in enough troops (the effect of which is not so much to frighten the bandit but to make the life of the peasants who support him miserable), and if a sufficiently large reward is offered, then his days are counted. Only modern, organized guerrilla war can resist under such conditions; but Robin Hoods are very far from modern guerrillas; partly because they operate as leaders of small bands, helpless outside their native territory, partly because they are organizationally and ideologically too archaic.

Indeed, they are not even social or any kind of revolutionaries, though the true Robin Hood sympathizes with the revolutionary aspirations of 'his' people and joins revolutions when he can. We shall consider this aspect of banditry in a later chapter. However, his object is comparatively modest. He protests not against the fact that peasants are poor and oppressed. He seeks to establish or to re-establish justice or 'the old ways', that is to say, fair dealing in a society of oppression. He rights wrongs. He does not seek to establish a society of freedom and equality. The stories that are told about him record modest triumphs: a widow's farm saved, a local tyrant killed, an imprisoned man set free, an unjust death avenged. At most – and the case is rare enough – he may, like Vardarelli in Apulia, order bailiffs to give bread to their labourers, to permit the poor to glean, or he may distribute salt free, i.e. to cancel taxes. (This is an important function, which is why professional smugglers like Mandrin, the hero of eighteenth-century French bandit-myth, may acquire the Robin Hood halo without difficulty.)

The ordinary Robin Hood can do little more, though, as we shall see, there are societies in which banditry appears not simply in the form of the occasional hero who gathers about him the usual six to twenty men, but as a permanently established institution. In such countries the revolutionary potential

---

* Janošik lasted two years, Diego Corrientes three, Musolino two, most of the south Italian brigands of the 1860s not more than two, but Giuliano (1922–50) seven, until he lost the goodwill of the Mafia.

of robbers is considerably greater (see Chapter 5). The traditional 'noble robber' represents an extremely primitive form of social protest, perhaps the most primitive there is. He is an individual who refuses to bend his back, that is all. Most men of his kind will, in non-revolutionary conditions, be sooner or later tempted to take the easy road of turning into a simple robber who preys on the poor as well as the rich (except perhaps in his native village), a retainer of the lords, a member of some strong-arm squad which comes to terms with the structures of official power. That is why the few who do not, or who are believed to have remained uncontaminated, have so great and passionate a burden of admiration and longing laid upon them. They cannot abolish oppression. But they do prove that justice is possible, that poor men need not be humble, helpless and meek.*

That is why Robin Hood cannot die, and why he is invented even when he does not really exist. Poor men have need of him, for he represents justice, without which, as Saint Augustine observed, kingdoms are nothing but great robbery. That is why they need him most, perhaps, when they cannot hope to overthrow oppression, but merely seek its alleviation, even when they half-accept the law which condemns the brigand, who yet represents divine justice and a higher form of society which is powerless to be born:

> I the scriptures have fulfilled,
> Though a wicked life I led
> When the naked I beheld
> I've clothed them and fed;
> Sometime in a coat of winter's pride,
> Sometime in russet grey,
> The naked I've clothed and the hungry I've fed,
> And the rich I've sent empty away.[21]

---

* It is significant that the leaders of legendary bands are often presented as personally weak or defective and are rarely supposed to be the strongest members of their band. 'For the Lord wished to prove by his example that all of us, everyone that is frightened, humble and poor, can do great deeds if God will have it so.

6. Robert Mandrin, the smuggler who was cast for the role of 'noble' robber and popular hero in eighteenth-century France.

# 4

# The Avengers

God himself almost repents
Having made the human race,
For all is injustice,
Affliction and vanity,
And man, however pious,
Cannot but regard as cruel
The supreme Majesty.

*Brazilian bandit-romance.*[1]

Ah gentlemen, if I had been able to read and write, I'd have destroyed
the human race.

*Michele Caruso, shepherd and bandit,*
*captured at Benevento 1863*

Moderation in killing and violence belongs to the image of the
social bandits. We need not expect them as a group to live up
to the moral standards they accept and their public expects
from them, any more than the ordinary citizen. Nevertheless it
is at first sight strange to encounter bandits who not only
practise terror and cruelty to an extent which cannot possibly
be explained as mere backsliding, but whose terror actually
forms part of their public image. They are heroes not in spite
of the fear and horror their actions inspire, but in some ways
because of them. They are not so much men who right wrongs,
but avengers, and exerters of power; their appeal is not that of
the agents of justice, but of men who prove that even the poor
and weak can be terrible.

Whether we ought to regard these public monsters as a
special sub-variety of social banditry, is not easy to say. The
moral world to which they belong (i.e. which finds expression
in the songs, poems and chapbooks about them) contains the
values of the 'noble robber' as well as those of the monster. As
the bush poet wrote of the great Lampião,

> He killed for play
> Out of pure perversity
> And gave food to the hungry
> With love and charity.

Among the *cangaçeiros* of the Brazilian north-east there are those, like the great Antonio Silvino (1875–1944, fl. as bandit chief 1896–1914), who are mainly remembered for their good deeds, and others, like Rio Preto, mainly for their cruelty. However, broadly speaking, the 'image' of the *cangaçeiro* combines both. Let us illustrate this by following the account of one of the backwoods bards of the most celebrated *cangaçeiro*, Virgulino Ferreira da Silva (?1898–1938), universally known as 'The Captain' or 'Lampião'.

He was born, so the legend goes (and it is the image rather than the reality which interests us for the moment), of respectable cattle-raising and farming parents at the foot of the mountains in the dry backlands of Pernambuco State 'in that time of the past when the back country was pretty prosperous', an intellectual – and therefore in the legend not a particularly powerful – boy. The weak must be able to identify with the great bandit. As the poet Zabele wrote,

> Where Lampião lives
> Worms become brave
> The monkey fights the jaguar,
> The sheep stands his ground.

His uncle, Manoel Lopes, said this boy must become a doctor, which made people smile for

> Never was seen a doctor
> In that immense *sertão*;
> There men knew only cowhands,
> Bands of *cangaçeiros*
> Or ballad-singers.

Anyway, young Virgulino did not want to be a doctor but a *vaqueiro* or cowpuncher, though he learned his letters and the 'Roman algorism' after only three months at school and was

an expert poet. The Ferreiras were expelled by the Nogueiras
from their farm when he was seventeen, being falsely accused
of theft. That is how the feud began which was to make him
into an outlaw. 'Virgulino,' someone said, 'trust in the divine
judge,' but he answered: 'The good book says honour your
father and mother, and if I did not defend our name, I would
lose my manhood.' So

> He bought a rifle and dagger
> In the town of São Francisco

and formed a band with his brothers and twenty-seven other
fighters (known to the poet as to their neighbours by nicknames,
often traditional to those who took up the career of the bandit)
to attack the Nogueiras in the Serra Vermelha. From blood-
feud to outlawry was a logical – in view of the superior power
of the Nogueiras a necessary – step. Lampião became a roving
bandit, more famous even than Antonio Silvino, whose capture
in 1914 had left a void in the backwoods pantheon:

> He spared the skin
> Neither of soldier nor civilian,
> His darling was the dagger
> His gift was the gun ...
> He left the rich as beggars,
> The brave fell at his feet,
> While others fled the country.

But during all the years (in fact *c*. 1920–38) when he was the
terror of the north-east, he never ceased to deplore his fate,
says the poet, which had made him a robber instead of an
honest labourer, and destined him for certain death, tolerable
only if he had the luck to die in a fair fight.

He was and is a hero to the people, but an ambiguous one.
Normal caution might explain why the poet makes his bow to
formal morality and records the 'joy of the north' at the death
of the great bandit. (By no means all ballads take this view.)
The reaction of a backwoodsman in the township of Mosquito
is probably more typical. When the soldiers came by with
their victims' heads in jars of kerosene, so as to convince all

that Lampião was really dead, he said: 'They have killed the Captain, because strong prayer is no good in water'.[2] For his last refuge was in the dried bed of a stream, and how else except by the failure of his magic could his fall be explained? Nevertheless, though a hero, he was not a *good* hero.

It is true that he had made a pilgrimage to the famous Messiah of Juazeiro, Padre Cicero, asking his blessing before turning bandit, and that the saint, though exhorting him vainly to give up the outlaw's life, had given him a document appointing him captain, and his two brothers lieutenants.* However, the ballad from which I have taken most of this account does not mention any righting of wrongs (except those done to the band itself), no taking from the rich to give to the poor, no bringing of justice. It records battles, and wounds, raids on towns (or what passed for towns in the Brazilian backwoods), kidnappings, hold-ups of the rich, adventures with the soldiers, with women, with hunger and thirst, but nothing that recalls the Robin Hoods. On the contrary, it records 'horrors': how Lampião murdered a prisoner though his wife had ransomed him, how he massacred labourers, tortured an old woman who cursed him (not knowing whom she entertained) by making her dance naked with a cactus-bush until she died, how he sadistically killed one of his men who had offended him by making him eat a litre of salt, and similar incidents. To be terrifying and pitiless is a more important attribute of this bandit than to be the friend of the poor.

And curiously enough, though the real life Lampião was undoubtedly capricious and sometimes cruel, he saw himself as the upholder of right in at least one important respect: sexual morality.

Seducers were castrated, bandits forbidden to rape women (given the attractions of their calling, they would rarely need to), and public opinion in the band was shocked at the order to shave off a woman's hair and drive her naked away, even though she was being punished for treason. At least one member of the band, Angelo Roque, nicknamed Labarêda, who retired

* For the real basis of this story, see below p. 92.

to become doorkeeper at the Law Courts in Bahia (!!), seems to have had the genuine instincts of a Robin Hood. Yet these characteristics do not dominate in the myth.

Terror is indeed part of the image of numerous bandits:

> All the plain of Vich
> Trembles as I pass.

says the hero of one of the numerous ballads celebrating the Catalan *bandoleros* of the sixteenth and seventeenth centuries, in which 'episodes of generosity do not abound' (in the words of their excellent historian Fuster), though the popular heroes among them are in most other respects 'noble'. They become *bandoleros* through some non-criminal action, rob the rich and not the poor, must remain 'honourable' as they were at the outset, e.g. kill only 'in the discharge of honour'. Terror, as we shall see, is an integral part of the image of the haiduks, who do not give much to the poor either. Once again it is mixed with some characteristics of the 'noble robber'. Terror and cruelty, again, are combined with 'nobility' in the character of an entirely fictional desperado, Joaquin Murieta, who championed Mexicans against Yankees in early California – a literary invention, but one credible enough to have entered Californian folklore and even historiography. In all these cases the bandit is essentially a symbol of power and vengeance.

The examples of genuinely unqualified cruelty, on the other hand, are not normally those of characteristic bandits. It is perhaps a mistake to classify as banditry the epidemic of blood-lust which swept the Peruvian department of Huanuco from about 1917 to the late 1920s, for though robbery formed part of it, its motive is described as 'not exactly this, but rather hatred and blood-feud'. It was indeed, according to the evidence, a blood-feud situation which got out of hand, and produced that 'fever of death among men', which led them to 'burn, rape, kill, sack and destroy coldly' everywhere except in their native community or village. Even more obviously the ghastly phenomenon of the Colombian *violencia* of the years after 1948 goes far beyond ordinary social banditry. Nowhere is the element of pathological violence for its own sake more startling than in this peasant revolution aborted into anarchy, though some of the most terrible practices, such as that of chopping prisoners into tiny fragments 'in front of and for the entertainment of the fighting men crazed by barbarity' (later to be known as *picar a tamal*) are alleged to have occurred in earlier guerrilla campaigns in that bloodthirsty country.[3] The point to note about these epidemics of cruelty and massacre is that they are immoral even by the standards of those who participate in them. If the massacre of entire bus-loads of harmless passengers or villagers is comprehensible in the context of savage civil warfare, such (well-attested) incidents as ripping the foetus out of a pregnant woman and substituting a cock can only be conscious 'sins'. And yet, some of the men who perpetrate these monstrosities are and remain 'heroes' to the local population.

Excessive violence and cruelty are thus phenomena which only overlap banditry at certain points. Nevertheless, it is sufficiently significant to require some explanation *as a social phenomenon*. (That this or that individual bandit may be a psychopath is irrelevant; in fact, it is rather improbable that many peasant bandits are psychologically deranged.)

Two possible reasons can be accepted, but are not sufficient to account for the whole of ultra-violence. The first is that, in the words of the Turkish author Yashar Kemal, 'brigands live by love and fear. When they inspire only love, it is a weakness. When they inspire only fear, they are hated and have no supporters.'[4] In other words, even the best of bandits must demonstrate that he can be 'terrible'. The second is that cruelty is inseparable from vengeance, and vengeance is an entirely legitimate activity for the noblest of bandits. To make the oppressor pay for the humiliation inflicted on the victim in his own coin is impossible; for the oppressor acts within a framework of accepted wealth, power and social superiority which the victim cannot use, unless there has been a social revolution which unseats the mighty as a class and elevates the humble. He has only his private resources and among them violence and cruelty are the most visibly effective. Thus in the well-known

Bulgarian ballad of cruel banditry, 'Stoian and Nedelia', Stoian and the bandits raid the village in which he was once mistreated as Nedelia's hired servant. He kidnaps her and makes her the bandits' serving-maid, but the humiliation is not enough: he cuts off her head for revenge.

Clearly, however, there is more to the outbursts of apparently gratuitous cruelty than this. Two possible explanations may be suggested with some hesitation, for social psychology is a jungle into which only a fool ventures carelessly.

Several of the best-known examples of ultra-violence are associated with particularly humiliated and inferior groups (e.g. the coloured in societies of white racialism), or with the even more galling situation of minorities oppressed by majorities. Is is perhaps no accident that the creator of the noble but also notably cruel band of Joaquin Murieta, avenger of the Californian Mexicans against the conquering *gringos*, was himself a Cherokee Indian, that is to say a member of an even more hopelessly dominated minority group. Lopez Albujar, who has described the storm of blood which swept the Indian peasants of Huanuco (Peru), has seen the connection admirably. These 'bandits' robbed, burned and murdered, at bottom 'in retaliation against the insatiable rapacity of all men who did not belong to their race', i.e. the whites. The occasional savage *jacqueries* of the Indian serfs against their white masters in Bolivia, before the revolution of 1952, show similar (temporary) shifts from the normal stolid passivity of the peasant to cruel fury.

A wild and indiscriminate retaliation: yes, but perhaps also, and especially among the weak, the permanent victims who have no hope of real victory even in their dreams, a more general 'revolution of destruction', which tumbles the whole world in ruins, since no 'good' world seems possible. Stagolee, the mythical hero of the Negro ballad, destroys the entire city like an earthquake, another Samson. Brecht's Pirate Jenny, the lowest kitchenmaid in the sleaziest hotel, the victim of all who meet her, dreams of the pirates who will come in their eight-sailed ship, capture the city, and ask her who shall be spared.

None shall be spared, they must all die, and Pirate Jenny will joke as their heads fall. Thus in the romances of the oppressed labourers of the Italian South the heroes of legend, such as the Calabrian bandit Nino Martino, dreamed of universal ruin. In such circumstances to assert power, any power, is itself a triumph. Killing and torture is the most primitive and personal assertion of ultimate power, and the weaker the rebel feels himself to be at bottom, the greater, we may suppose, the temptation to assert it.

But even when such rebels triumph, victory brings its own temptation to destroy, for primitive peasant insurgents have no positive programme, only the negative programme of getting rid of the superstructure which prevents men from living well and dealing fairly, as in the good old days. To kill, to slash, to burn away everything that is not necessary and useful to the man at the plough or with the herdsman's crook, is to abolish corruption and leave only what is good, pure and natural. Thus the brigand-guerrillas of the Italian South destroyed not only their enemies and the legal documents of bondage, but unnecessary riches. Their social justice was destruction.

There is, however, another situation in which violence passes the bounds of what is conventionally accepted even in habitually violent societies. This occurs during periods of rapid social change, which destroy the traditional mechanisms of social control holding destructive anarchy at bay. The phenomenon of feuds 'getting out of hand' is familiar to observers of societies regulated by blood vengeance. This is normally a social device containing its own automatic brake. Once the score between two feuding families is evened, by another death or some other compensation, a settlement is negotiated, guaranteed by third parties, by inter-marriage or in other well-understood ways, so that killing shall not proceed without end. Yet if for some reason (such as, most obviously, the intervention of the new-fangled state in some way incomprehensible to local custom, or by lending support to the more politically influential of the contending families) the brake ceases to function, feuds develop into those protracted mutual massacres which end either with the extirpation of one family or, after years of warfare, the return to the negotiated settlement which ought to have been made at the outset. As we have seen in the example of Lampião, such breakdowns in the customary mechanism of feud-settlement can among other things multiply outlaws and bandits (and indeed feud is the almost invariable starting-point of a Brazilian *cangaçeiro's* career).

We have some excellent examples of more general breakdowns in such customary devices of social control. In his admirable autobiography *Land Without Justice*, Milovan Djilas describes the ruin of the system of values which governed the behaviour of men in his native Montenegro, after the First World War. And he records a strange episode. The Orthodox Montenegrins had always been accustomed, in addition to their internal feuding, to raid or be raided by their neighbours, the Catholic Albanians and the Moslem Bosnians. In the early 1920s a party set out to raid the Bosnian villages as men had done from time immemorial. To their own horror they discovered themselves to be doing things which raiders had never done before and which they knew to be wrong: torturing, raping, murdering children. *And they could not help themselves.* The rules men lived by had once been clearly understood; their rights and obligations, like the scope, the limits, the times and the objects of their actions were established by custom and precedent. They were compelling not only for this reason but because they were part of a system, and one whose elements did not conflict too obviously with reality. One part of the system had broken down: they could no longer regard themselves as 'heroes' since (if we follow Djilas's argument) they had not fought to the death against the Austrian conquest. Hence the other parts ceased also to operate: when going out to fight they could no longer behave as 'heroes'. Not until the heroic system of values was restored on a new and more viable basis – paradoxically enough by the mass adhesion of the Montenegrins to the Communist Party – did the society recover its 'mental balance'. When the call for a rising against the Germans went out in 1941, thousands of men with rifles went into the Montenegrin hills to fight, kill and die 'honourably' once again.*

Banditry, we have seen, grows and becomes epidemic in times of social tension and upheaval. These are also the times when the conditions for such explosions of cruelty are most favourable. They do not belong to the central image of brigandage, except insofar as the bandit is at all times an avenger of the poor. But at such times they will no doubt occur more frequently and systematically. Nowhere more so than in those peasant insurrections and rebellions which have failed to turn into social revolutions, and whose militants are forced to fall back into the life of outlaws and robbers: hungry, embittered and resentful even against the poor who have left them to fight alone. Or, what is even worse, among that second generation of 'children of violence' who graduate from the ashes of their homes, the corpses of their fathers and the raped bodies of their mothers and sisters to the life of outlawry:

'What has impressed you most?
Seeing the houses burn.
What made you suffer most?
My mother and my little brothers weeping for hunger on the mountain.
Have you been wounded?
Five times, all rifle shots.
What would you like most?
Let them leave me in peace and I shall work. I want to learn to read.
But all they want is to kill me. I'm not one they will leave alive.'[5]

The speaker is the Colombian band chieftain Teofilo Rojas ('Chispas'), aged twenty-two and at the time of this interview charged with about four hundred crimes: thirty-seven massacred in Romerales, eighteen in Altamira, eighteen in Chili, thirty in San Juan de la China and again in El Salado, twenty-five in Toche and again in Guadual, fourteen in Los Naranjos and so on.

*The Montenegrins, 1·4% of the Yugoslav population, provided 17% of the officers in the Partisan army.

Monsignor German Guzman, who knows the *violencia* of his native Colombia better than most, has described these lost and murderous children of anarchy. For them

In the first place man and land, so essentially tied together in the peasant's life, have been torn apart. They do not till the soil nor care for the trees. . . . They are men, or rather adolescents, without hope. Uncertainty surrounds their lives, which find expression in adventure, self-realization in mortal undertakings, which have no transcendental meaning. Second, they have lost the sense of the farm as an anchor, a place to love, from which to draw tranquillity, a feeling of security and permanence. They are forever itinerant adventurers and vagabonds. Instability and the loosening of bonds come with outlawry. For them to halt, to grow fond of a place, would be the equivalent of giving themselves up; it would be the end. Thirdly, their rootless lives take these young enemies of society into temporary, precarious and insecure environments very different from those of the lost home. Their nomadic life implies a disordered search for the occasions of emotional satisfaction, for which they no longer have a stable framework. Here lies the key to their sexual anxiety and the pathological frequency of their aberrant crimes. For them love means most commonly rape or casual concubinage. . . . When they think the girls want to leave them for any reason, they kill them. Fourthly, they lose the sense of the *path* as an element that integrates peasant life. The highlander cares for the paths along which men carry their countless loads, until in a sense they become his own intimate possession. It is a sort of love which makes men invariably come and go along them. But the anti-social bandit of our day leaves the known footpath, because the soldiers pursue him, or because guerrilla tactics compel him to seek places for unsuspected ambush or secret tracks to the surprise assault.[6]

Only a firm ideology and discipline can prevent men degenerating into wolves under such circumstances, but neither are characteristics of the grass-roots rebel.

Still, though we must mention the pathological aberrations of banditry, the violence and cruelty which is most permanent and characteristic is the one which is inseparable from revenge. Revenge for personal humiliation, but also revenge on those who have oppressed others. In May 1744 the bandit captain Oleksa Dovbuš attacked the seat of Konstantin Zlotnicky, Gentleman. He held his hands in the fire and let them burn, poured glowing coals on his skin and refused any ransom. 'I have not come for ransom but for your soul, for you have tortured the people long enough'; so the Cistercian monks of Lwow report him. He also killed Zlotnicky's wife and half-grown son. The chronicle of the monks concludes its entry with the observation that Zlotnicky had been a cruel lord, who had in his time caused many to be killed. Where men become bandits, cruelty breeds cruelty, blood calls for blood.[7]

# 5
# Haiduks

Nemtcho has become an orphan,
without father, without mother,
and on earth he has no person
to give counsel, to direct him,
how to till and how to harvest
on the land his father left him.
But instead he is a haiduk,
standard-bearer of the haiduks,
and the keeper of their treasure.

*Haiduk ballad.*[1]

In the mountains and empty plains of south-eastern Europe the
advance of Christian landlords and Turkish conquerors made
life increasingly burdensome for the peasants from the fifteenth
century on but, unlike more densely settled or firmly administered regions, left a broad margin of potential freedom. Groups
and communities of free, armed and combative men therefore
emerged among those expelled from their lands or escaping
from serfdom, at first almost spontaneously, later in organized
forms. What a scholar has called 'military strata sprung from
the free peasantry' therefore became characteristic of this large
zone, groups called Cossacks in Russia, *klephtes* in Greece,
*haidamaks* in Ukraine, but in Hungary and the Balkan penin-
sula north of Greece mainly haiduks (*hajdú, hajdut, hajdutin*),
a word of either Turkish or Magyar origin whose philology
and original meaning is as usual hotly disputed. They were a
collective form of that individual peasant dissidence which, as
we have seen, produced the classical bandits.

As with the men among whom Robin Hoods and avengers
were recruited, haiduks were not automatically committed to
rebellion against all authority. They could, as in some parts of
Hungary, become attached to lords whom they provided with

fighters against a recognition of their status as free men. By a natural development of reality and language the term '*heiduck*' describing the free robber-liberator *par excellence* could thus also become the term for one of the numerous types of flunkey of the German nobility. More commonly, as in Russia and Hungary, they accepted land from the emperor or tsar or other prince against the obligation to maintain arms and horses, and to fight the Turk under chieftains of their own choosing, and thus became the guardians of the military frontier, a sort of rank-and-file knighthood. Nevertheless, they were essentially free – as such superior to and contemptuous of servile peasants, but constant magnets to rebel and runaway elements, and with a far from unconditional loyalty. The great peasant revolts of seventeenth- and eighteenth-century Russia all began on the Cossack frontier.

There was, however, a third type of haidukdom, which refused to attach itself to any Christian noble or ruler, if only because in the area in which it flourished most nobles and rulers were unbelieving Turks. Neither royal nor signorial, these free haiduks were robbers by trade, enemies of the Turks and popular avengers by social role, primitive movements of guerrilla resistance and liberation. As such they appear in the fifteenth century, possibly first in Bosnia and Herzegovina, but later all over the Balkans and Hungary, most notably in Bulgaria, where a '*haidot*' chieftain is recorded as early as 1454. These are the men whose name I have chosen to typify the highest form of primitive banditry, the one which comes closest to being a permanent and conscious focus of peasant insurrection. Such 'haiduks' existed not only in south-eastern Europe, but under other names in various other parts of the world, e.g. Indonesia and, most notably, Imperial China. For obvious reasons they were most common among peoples oppressed by conquerors of foreign language or religion, but not only there.

Ideology or class-consciousness was not normally the motive which drove men to become haiduks, and even the sort of non-criminal troubles which drove individual bandits into outlawry were not particularly common. We have examples of this kind, such as the Bulgarian haiduk chieftain Panayot Hitov (who has left us an invaluable autobiography), who took to the mountains at the age of twenty-five after a fight with a Turkish law official, arising out of some obscure legal trouble, in the 1850s. In general, however, if we are to believe the innumerable haiduk songs and ballads which are one of the chief sources for our knowledge of this type of banditry, the motive to become a haiduk was strictly economic. The winter was bad, says one such song, the summer was parched, the sheep died. So Stoian became a haiduk:

> Whoever wants to become a free haiduk,
> step this way, stand up beside me.
> twenty lads thus came together,
> And we'd nothing, not a thing between us,
> no sharp swords, but only sticks.[2]

Conversely, Tatuncho the haiduk returned to the family holding because his mother pleaded with him, and anyway she said a robber could not feed his family. But the sultan sent his soldiers to capture him. He killed them all and brought the money in their belts back: 'There's the money, mother, who will say that a bandit does not feed his mother?' In fact, with luck brigandage was a better financial proposition than peasant life.

Under the circumstances pure social banditry was rare. Panayot Hitov singles out one such rarity in his proud survey of the celebrated practitioners of the calling which he himself adorned: a certain Doncho Vatach, who flourished in the 1840s, only persecuted Turkish evildoers, helped the Bulgarian poor and distributed money. The classical 'noble robber' of Bulgaria, observed the British authors of *A Residence in Bulgaria* (1869), as so often inclined to sympathize with Islamic heroism, were the *chelibi*, normally 'well-born' Turks, as distinct from the *khersis* or ordinary robbers, who enjoyed the sympathy of their villages, and the haiduks, who were murdering outlaws, cruel by nature and unsupported except in their own band. This may be an exaggeration, but certainly the haiduks were not Robin Hoods, and their victims were anyone they could catch. The ballads are full of variations on the phrase

> We have made many mothers weep,
> We have widowed many wives,
> Many more have we made orphans,
> For we are childless men ourselves.

Haiduk cruelty is a familiar theme. Unquestionably the haiduk was far more permanently cut off from the peasantry than the classical social bandit, not only masterless but also – at least during their bandit career – often kinless men ('without mothers all, and without sisters'), living with the peasantry not so much like Mao's proverbial fish in water, but rather like soldiers who leave their village for the semi-permanent exile of army life. A rather high proportion of them were in any case herdsmen and drovers, i.e. semi-migratory men whose links with the settlements are intermittent or tenuous. It is significant that the Greek *klephtes* (and perhaps the Slav haiduks also) had their special language or argot.

The distinction between robber and hero, between what the peasant would accept as 'good' and condemn as 'bad', was therefore exceptionally difficult, and haiduk songs insist on their sins as often as on their virtues, as the famous Chinese Water Margin novel insists on the inhumanity (expressed in the familiar anecdotes of several who eventually join the large and variegated company of the heroic outlaws).* The definition of the haiduk-hero is fundamentally political. In the Balkans he was a *national* bandit, according to certain traditional rules, i.e. a defender or avenger of Christians against Turks. Insofar as he fought against the oppressor, his image was positive, though his actions might be black and his sins might lead him to eventual repentance as a monk, or punish him with nine years' illness. Unlike the 'noble robber', the haiduk does not

* However, I do not know of any haiduks who are accused of the anthropophagic practices – most commonly the slaughtering of travellers whose meat is sold to butchers – which the public seems to reserve for criminals genuinely regarded as outside normal society.

depend on personal moral approval; unlike the 'avenger' his cruelty is not his essential characteristic, but tolerated because of his services to the people.

What made this collection of the socially marginal, the men who chose not so much freedom as against serfdom, but robbery as against poverty, into a quasi-political movement, was a powerful tradition, a recognized collective social function. As we have seen, their motives for going into the mountains were

7. Mountain passes are familiar backgrounds for brigands – in this case Bulgarian haiduks.

mainly economic, but the technical term for becoming a haiduk was 'to rebel', and the haiduk was by definition an insurrectionary. He joined a recognized social group. Without Robin Hood the merry men in Sherwood Forest are insignificant, but 'the haiduks' in the Balkans, like 'the bandits' on the Chinese mountain beyond the lake, are always there to receive the dissident or the outlaw. Their chieftains change, and some of them are more celebrated or nobler than others, but neither the existence nor the fame of the haiduks depends on the reputation of any single man. To this extent they are a socially recognized collection of heroes, and indeed, so far as I can tell, the protagonists of the haiduk ballad-cycles are not the men who became famous chieftains in real life, but the anonymous – or rather those called simply Stoian or Ivantcho like any peasant; not even necessarily the leaders of bands. The klephtic ballads of Greece are both less anonymous and less socially informative, belonging as they do to the literature of the praise (and self-praise) of professional fighting men. Their heroes are almost by definition celebrated figures, known to one and all.

Permanent existence went with formal structure and organization. The organization and hierarchy of the great brigand republic which is the subject of the Chinese Water Margin novel, is extremely elaborate; and not only because it has, unlike the illiterate lands of Europe, an honoured place for the ex-civil-servant and the displaced intellectual. (In fact, one of its main themes is the replacement of a low-grade intellectual bandit chief – one of those failed examination-candidates who were so obvious a source of political dissidence in the heavenly empire – by a successful intellectual one; as it were the triumph of the first-class mind.) Haiduk bands were led by (elected) *voivodes* or dukes, whose duty was to supply arms assisted by a standard-bearer or *bairaktar*, who carried the red or green banner and also acted as treasurer and quartermaster. We find a similar military structure and terminology among the Russian *rasboiniki* and in some of the Indian dacoit communities, as among the Sansia, whose bands of *sipahis* (*sepoys, spahis*= soldiers) were led by Jemadars, who received two shares of loot for every one distributed to the ranker, but also ten per cent of the total for the provision of torches, spears and other tools of the trade.*

---

* Indian dacoits were generally classified as either 'criminal castes' or 'criminal tribes' by the British. But behind the familiar Indian penchant for

Haiduk banditry was therefore in every respect a more serious, a more ambitious, permanent and institutionalized challenge to official authority than the scattering of Robin Hoods or other robber rebels which emerged from any normal peasant society. It is not easy to say whether this was so because certain geographical or political conditions made possible such permanent and formalized banditry, and therefore automatically made it potentially more 'political', or whether it was certain political situations (e.g. foreign conquest or certain types of social conflict) which encouraged unusually 'conscious' forms of banditry and thus structured it more firmly and permanently. Both, we may say, begging the question, though it still requires an answer. I do not think that the individual haiduk would have been able to give it, for he would rarely if ever be able to step outside the social and cultural frame which enclosed him and his people. Let us try and draw a brief portrait-sketch of him.

He would see himself, above all, as a free man – and as such as good as a lord or king; a man who had in this sense won personal emancipation and therefore superiority. The *klephtes* on Mount Olympus who captured the respectable Herr Richter, prided themselves on their equality to kings, and rejected certain kinds of behaviour as 'un-royal', and therefore improper. Just so the north Indian Badhaks claimed that 'our profession has been a king's trade', and – at least in theory – accepted the obligations of chivalry, such as not insulting females, and killing only in fair fight, though we may regard it as certain

---

giving every social and occupational group its separate social identity – i.e. what is vulgarly called the 'caste system' – we can often detect something not unlike haidukdom. Thus the most celebrated of the north Indian bandit 'tribes', the Badhaks, were originally outcasts of Moslem and Hindu provenance, 'a sort of Cave of Adullam for the reception of vagrants and bad characters of different tribes'; the Sansia, though perhaps developed from among hereditary bards and genealogists – they still held this function among some Rajputs at the end of the nineteenth century – freely accepted outside recruits into their community; and the formidable Minas of central India are supposed to have been dispossessed peasants and village watchmen who took to the hills and became professional brigands.

that few haiduks could actually afford to fight in this noble manner. Freedom implied equality among haiduks and there are some impressive examples of it. For instance, when the King of Oudh tried to form a regiment of Badhaks, much as the Russian and Austrian emperors formed haiduk and Cossack units, they mutinied because the officers had refused to perform the same duties as the men. Such behaviour is unusual enough, but in a society so imbued with caste inequality as the Indian, it almost passes belief.

Haiduks were always free men, but in the typical case of the Balkan haiduks they were not free communities. For the *četa* or band, being essentially a voluntary union of individuals who cut themselves off from their kin, was automatically an abnormal social unit, since it lacked wives, children and land. It was doubly 'unnatural', for often the haiduk's road back to ordinary civilian life in his own native village was barred by the Turks. The haiduk ballads sing of the men whose swords were their only sisters, whose rifles their wives, and who would shake hands silently and sadly as the *četa* broke up, to disperse as lost individuals to the four corners of the earth. Death was their equivalent of marriage, and the ballads constantly speak of it as such. Normal forms of social organization were therefore not available to them, any more than to soldiers on campaigns, and unlike the great bands of marauding *krdžali** of the late eighteenth and early nineteenth century, who carried with them male and female harems in the usual Turkish manner, the haiduks made no attempts to establish families while they were haiduks; perhaps because their units were too small to defend them. If they had any model of social organization, it was the male brotherhood or society, of which the famous Zaporozhe Cossacks are the best known example.

This anomaly comes out clearly in their relation to women. Haiduks like all bandits had nothing whatever against them. Quite the contrary, for as a confidential report on a Mace-

---

*Troops of disbanded soldiers and desperadoes who roamed Bulgaria at the end of the eighteenth century.

donian *komitadji*\* chief observed in 1908, 'like almost all *voivodes*, he is a great lover of women'.³ Girls – curiously enough in the ballads some seem to have been Bulgarian Jewesses – sometimes joined the haiduks and occasionally some Boyana, Yelenka or Todorka even became a *voivode*. Some returned, after a ceremonial farewell, to ordinary life and marriage:

> Penka went on to the mountains,
> On the mountain to the haiduks,
> For she wanted to bring gifts
> For her time had come to marry:
> To each soldier she gave a handkerchief,
> In each cloth a piece of gold,
> That the haiduks should remember
> When their Penka had got wed.⁴

But it seems that for the time of their haiduk life, these runaway girls were men, dressed in men's clothes, and fighting like men. The ballad tells of the girl who returned home to the woman's role, because her mother urged her, but could not stand it, put away her spindle and took up her rifle again to be a haiduk man. Just as freedom meant noble status for a man, it meant male status for a woman. Conversely, in theory at least, on the mountains haiduks avoided sex with women. The klephtic ballads insist on the enormity of touching women prisoners held for ransom or other purposes, and both they and the Bulgarian outlaws held the belief that one who attacked a woman was inevitably caught, that is to say tortured and killed by the Turks. The belief is significant, even if (as we may well suspect) the outlaws fell short of it in practice.⁵ In non-haiduk bands, women are known, but not common. Lampião seems to have been the only Brazilian leader who let them share the roving life; probably after he fell in love with the beautiful Maria Bonita, an affair much celebrated in the ballads. This was noted as exceptional.

Of course it might not limit them excessively, for, like the usual robber's life, the haiduk's was seasonal. 'They have a

\* Guerrillas established by the Supreme Committee for Macedonia and Adrianople of the Macedonian revolutionaries.

proverb', wrote an eighteenth-century German of the Dalma-
tian Morlacks, '*Jurwew dance, aiducki sastance*, come St
George's day, up haiduks and gather round (for then robberies are made easier by the green leaves and the abundance
of travellers)'.[6] The Bulgarian haiduks buried their arms on
the day of the Cross on 14/27 September until St George's Day
next spring. Indeed what could haiduks do in winter when there
was nobody to rob except villagers? The hardiest might take
supplies into their mountain caves, but it would be more convenient to winter in some friendly village, singing heroic songs
and drinking, and if the season had been poor – for how much
was there to rob on the by-roads of Macedonia or Herzegovina
at the best of times? – they might take service with rich
peasants. Or else they might return to their kin, for in some
highland areas there were 'few large families which did not send
some of their members among the haiduks'.[7] If the outlaws
lived as strict male brotherhoods, recognizing no bonds except
those of the 'true and united band of comrades' it was only for
the campaigning season.

Thus they lived their wild, free lives in the forest, the mountain caves, or on the wide steppes, armed with the 'rifle as tall
as a man', the pair of pistols at the belt, the *yatagan*\* and 'sharp
Frankish sword', their tunics laced, gilded and criss-crossed by
bandoleers, their moustaches bristling, conscious that fame was
their reward among enemies and friends. The mythology of
heroism, the ritualization of the ballad, turned them into type-
figures. We know little or nothing about Novak and his sons
Grujo and Radivoj, about Mihat the herdsman, Rado of Sokol,
Bujadin, Ivan Visnic and Luka Golowran except that they
were celebrated Bosnian haiduks of the nineteenth century,
because those who sang about them (including themselves) did
not have to tell their public what the lives of Bosnian peasants
and herdsmen were like. Only occasionally does the cloud of
heroic anonymity lift, and a haiduk career emerge at least
partly into the light of history.

---

\*Mohammedan sword without guard to handle, often with a double-
curved blade.

Such a one is that of the *voivode* Korčo, the son of a shepherd from near Strumica (in Macedonia), who served a Turkish
Beg. An epidemic killed the flock, and the Beg imprisoned the
father. The son went into the mountains to threaten the Turk,
but in vain: the old man died in jail. At the head of a haiduk
band Korčo then captured a young Turkish 'nobleman', broke
his arms and legs, cut off his head and paraded it through the
Christian villages on a lance. After that he was a haiduk for
ten years, until he bought some mules, exchanged haiduk costume for the merchant's and vanished – at least from the world
of heroic memories – for another ten. At the end of this time
he appeared at the head of three hundred men (let us not in-
quire too closely into the rounded numbers of epics) and took
service with the redoubtable Pasvan (Osman Pasvanoglu, a
Mohammedan Bosnian who became Pasha of Vidin), who was
in opposition to the Sublime Porte and led the savage formations of *krdžali* against the Sultan's more loyal servants. Korčo
did not stay long in the service of Pasvan. Setting off on his
own again he attacked and captured the town of Strumica, not
only because peasant haiduks hated and distrusted cities, but
because it sheltered the Beg who had caused his father's death.
He killed the Beg and massacred the population. Then he returned to Vidin and history or legend loses track of him. His
end is unknown. Since the era of the *krdžali* raids was, approxi-
mately, the 1790s and 1800s, his career can be roughly dated.
His story is told by Panayot Hitov.

Their existence was its own justification. It proved that oppression was not universal, and vengeance for oppression was
possible. Hence the peasants and herdsmen in the haiduks'
own home region identified with them. We need not suppose
that they spent all their time fighting, let alone trying to overthrow, the oppressors. The very existence of bands of free men,
or of those small patches of rock or reed beyond the reach of
any administration, was sufficient achievement. Those Greek
mountains proudly called Agrapha (the 'unwritten', because
nobody had ever succeeded in enrolling their population for
taxes) were independent in practice if not in law. So haiduks

1. Dick Turpin 'as he concealed himself in a cave in Epping Forest'.
Engraving by J. Smith, 1739.

# Robin Hood's Golden Prize.

He met two Priests upon the way,
And forced them with him to Pray,
For Gold they pray'd, and Gold they had,
Enough to make bold *Robin* glad :
His share came to four hundred pound
That then was told upon the ground:
Now mark and you shall here the jest,
You never heard the like exprest.

Tune is, *Robin Hood was a tall young man.*

I Have heard talk of bold Robin Hood,
 derry, derry down,
And of brave Little John,
Of Fryer Tuck, and William Scarlet,
Loxley, and Maid Marion,
 hey down, derry, derry down.
But such a tale as this, before
 derry, &c.
I think there was never none,
For Robin Hood disguised himself,
 and to the green wood is gone.
 hey down, &c.

Like to a Fryer bold Robin Hood
 derry, &c.
Was accoutred in his array,
With hood, gown, beads, and crucifix,
 he past upon the way.
 hey down, &c.

He had not gone miles two or three
 derry, &c.
But it was his chance to spy
Two lusty Priests clad all in black
 come riding gallantly.
 hey down, &c.

Benedicite then said Robin Hood,
 derry, &c.
Some pitty on me take,
Cross you my hand with a silver groat,
 for our dear Ladies sake.
 hey down, &c.

For I been wandring all this day,
 derry, &c.
And nothing could I get,
Not so much as one poor cup of drink,
 nor bit of bread to eat :
 hey down, &c.

Now by our holy dame the Priests re-
 derry, &c.          (ply'd,
We never a penny have,
For we this morning have been rob'd,
 and could no money save :
 hey down, &c.

I am afraid, said Robin Hood,
 derry, &c.
That you both do tell a lye,
And now before you no go hence
 I am resolv'd to try.
 hey down, &c.

When as the Priests heard him say so,
 derry, derry, &c.
They rode away amain,
But Robin Hood betook him to his heels
 and soon overtook them again.
 hey down, &c.

Then Robin Hood laid hold on them both
 derry, &c.
And pul'd them down from their horse,
O spare us fryer, the Priests cry'd out,
 on us have some remorse.
 hey down, derry, derry down.

2. Robin Hood transformed 1: a ballad sheet probably dating from the last third of the seventeenth century.

3. Robin Hood transformed 2: an engraving of *c.* 1700.

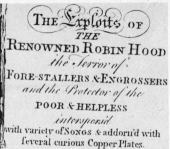

4. Robin Hood transformed 3: chapbook published in 1769. Hood and his mother 'entertained by Squire Gamwell at Gamwell Hall' have been absorbed by eighteenth-century England.

5. Robin Hood transformed 4: Errol Flynn in the role of the noble outlaw, as assimilated by Hollywood.

6. Monarch of the glen: the harshness of Highland outlawry softened down for the Victorian public on the title-page of a sheet of dance music.

Cartouche stielt eine Sack Uhr | Sein Camerad kompt in verhafft

Derwald ist mit Soldaten umbgebē | Läst in Paris Zettel anschlagen | Er mor

7. Louis-Dominique Cartouche (born Paris ?1693, executed 1721), the most famous gangster of his time, much celebrated in popular literature and iconography.

8. A contemporary German broadsheet on Cartouche, illustrating his exploits, pursuit, arrest and imprisonment. The imagery is that normally surrounding the urban criminal.

9. 'Schinderhannes' (J. Bückler 1783–1803), a criminal-robber who acquired the halo of social bandit among the Rhineland peasantry, shown robbing a Jew.

10. The execution of 'Schinderhannes', from a German popular biography. Note the traditional 'dying declaration' pose.

11. The bandit in high literature. Title-page of the first edition of Schiller's drama *The Robbers*.

# Die
# Räuber.

## Ein Schauspiel.

Frankfurt und Leipzig,
1781.

12. Modern Corsican bandits. N. Romanetti (1884–1926) of Vizzanova succeeded Bellacoscia, who was killed fighting, as the leading bandit of the island. Top right: an earlier bandit wearing traditional stocking cap (Phrygian bonnet).

13. The *bandolero* unromanticized: Goya's *Bandits attacking a coach* (*c.* 1792–1800). The painter treated this subject several times.

14. The *bandolero* romanticized by John Haynes Williams (1836–1908), whose every picture told a Victorian story, often about Spanish bandits and bullfighters.

15. Sicilian theatre puppets: on the right, the famous bandit Pasquale Bruno (subject of a novel by Dumas *père*). Bandits supplemented the Paladins of France in the puppet repertoire of the nineteenth century.

EX VOTO

16. Popular view of banditry in Catalonia. Ex-voto from Ripoll (Gerona province) showing the habitual armed men in the habitual mountains.

17. Sicilian terracotta group (Caltagirone, probably by F. Bonnano, who specialized in bandit themes). A wealthy land owner kidnapped. Note the traditional cloaks and comical caps of the brigands.

18. Sicilian peasant wood-carving from Syracuse province, mid-nineteenth century. In the centre are two bandits tied together, and on either side gendarmes mounted and on foot.

19. Giuseppe Musolino. Born in 1875 in San Stefano, Aspromonte, he was wrongly imprisoned in 1897, escaped in 1899, and was recaptured in 1901. He was in jail for forty-five years, where he went mad and died in 1956. He was immensely popular and famous far beyond his native Calabria.

20. Bandit territory: the Barbagia in Sardinia. From De Seta's film *Banditi ad Orgosolo* (1961), which reconstructs the making of a bandit from this legendary centre of outlaws.

21. The brigand romanticized by Charles-Alphonse-Paul Bellay (1826–1900), a copious exhibitor at the Paris Salon, with a *penchant* for picturesque Italian popular types.

22. Salvatore Giuliano (1922–50) alive. The most celebrated bandit of
the Italian republic was much, and flatteringly, photographed by
journalists.

23. Salvatore Giuliano dead, 5 July 1950, in a courtyard at Castelvetrano. The police, improbably, claimed credit for the killing. Note the pistol and the Bren gun.

24. Salvatore Giuliano. An ambush by the gang reconstructed in Francesco de Rosi's magnificent film, *Salvatore Giuliano*. The locations are actual.

25. Sardinia in the 1960s. Posters of bandits wanted by the police, with rewards ranging from two to ten million lire a head. Banditry is still endemic in the Barbagia highlands.

26. The James boys as heroes of popular fiction (Chicago, 1892).
Perhaps their habit of holding up trains helped to spread their fame.

27. A photograph of Jesse James (1847–82), with his brother Frank (1843–1915) the most famous actor of the social bandit role in U.S. history. He was born and died in Missouri. He formed his band after the Civil War (1866).

28. Jesse James as part of the Western legend. Henry Fonda in the film *Jesse James* (1939, Henry King).

HISTORIAS DO NORTE

A VIDA DE LAMPEÃO

1ª SÉRIE: - Infância, Juventude e Amores do Rei do Cangaço

Por: - ANTONIO TEODORO DOS SANTOS

29. Lampião (also spelt Lampeão, 1898–1938), the great bandit-hero of Brazil. Title-page of the first part of a three-part verse romance by a north-eastern balladeer, published in São Paulo (1962).

30. The bandit as national myth, propagated by intellectuals: a still from the Brazilian film *O Cangaçeiro* (1953). The decorated leather hats with upturned brims are the local equivalent of the sombrero or stetson.

31. 'Pancho' Villa (born in 1877 in Durango, died in 1923 in Chihuahua). The brigand as revolutionary general, December 1913.

Поллиппое изображеше
Бунтовщика и обманщика.
ЕМЕЛЬКІ ПУГАЧЕВА.

Wahre Abbildung
des Rebellen und Betrügers
IEMELKA PUGATSCEW.

22. An eighteenth-century engraving of the Cossack revolutionary:
Yemelyan Pugachov (1726–75), leader of the vast popular revolt of
1773–5. He came from the same village as Stepan Razin, bandit-leader of
the revolt of 1667–71, and hero of folksong.

33. The haiduk revolutionary: a photograph of Panayot Hitov (1830–1918), Bulgarian outlaw, patriot and autobiographer, leader of the national rising of 1867–8.

34. The klephtic image: Giorgios Volanis (centre), leader of Greek bands in Macedonia in the early 1900s. Note the warrior's ornaments.

Ο Έλλην αξχηγός Καραλίναι, Βολίναις, κτι Μαξιξε...

35. Balkan irregulars: Constantine Garefis, with his band (recruited around Olympus) c. 1905. He was killed by the Macedonian *Komitadjis* in 1906.

36. The bandit of the plains: a nineteenth-century lithograph of Sandor Rósza (1813–78), the Great Hungarian brigand-guerilla, in jail. A band-leader from *c.* 1841, a national guerilla after 1849, he was captured in 1856 and pardoned in 1867.

37. Sandor Rósza as legend: a scene from Miklos Jancso's film *The Round-Up*, which deals with the pursuit of Rósza by the imperial authorities.

38. Wu Sung commander of infantry of a bandit army in the famous Water Margin Novel, in a sixteenth-century illustration. He became an outlaw through a vengeance killing. He was described as 'tall, handsome, powerful, heroic, expert in military arts' and drink.

Chieh Chen, a rank-and-file bandit from the Water Margin Novel probably based on earlier themes. He came from Shantung, an orphan and a hunter, and was described as tall, tanned, slim and hot-tempered.

39. Execution of Namoa Pirates, Kowloon 1891, with British sahibs.
Namoa, an island off Swatow, was a great centre for piracy and, at this
time, the scene of a rebellion. We do not know whether the corpses had
been pirates, rebels or both.

40. Lolo tribal bandits from Szechuan province (China), chained together by caravans. Raiding was part of numerous frontier tribes' economics.

41. The Pindaris, described as 'a well-known professional class of freebooters', were associated with the Marathas in whose campaigns they took part, looting. After the British pacification the remainder settled down as cultivators.

# The Expropriators

42. 'Kamo' (Semyon Arzhakovich Ter-Petrossian), 1882–1922. A Bolshevik professional revolutionary from Armenia, he was noted as an immensely tough and courageous man of action. He was the instigator of the Tiflis hold-up of 1907.

43. 'El Quico' (Francisco Sabaté), 1913–60, Catalan anarchist and expropriator. The photo was taken in 1957 and shows him in frontier-crossing equipment.

# The Bandit in Art

44. The monumental bandit: *Heads of Brigands* by Salvator Rosa (1615–73).

5. The statuesque bandit: *Captain of Banditi* in an English
ighteenth-century engraving after Salvator Rosa.

theme by Francisco Goya y Lucrentes (1746–1828).

47. The sentimental bandit: *Bandit of the Apennines* (1824), by Sir Charles Eastlake (1793–1865), President of the Royal Academy.

48. The theatrical bandit: *Brigands* by Jean-Baptiste Thomas (1781–1854).

49. The operatic bandit: *The Brigand Betrayed*, by Jean-Émile-Horace Vernet (1789–1863, Légion d'Honneur 1862), a noted expert in exotic scenes adapted to a bourgeois public.

50. The bandit as symbol: *Ned Kelly* (1956) by Sidney Nolan. Part of a series about the famous bushranger (1854–80) with his home-made armour.

would raid. In the nature of their trade they would have to fight Turks (or whoever else represented authority), because it was authority's business to protect travelling goods and treasure. They would no doubt kill Turks with especial satisfaction, since they were unbelieving dogs and oppressors of good Christians, and perhaps also because fighting men are more heroic when they fight dangerous adversaries, whose bravery enhances their own. However, left to themselves there is no evidence that, say, the Balkan haiduks set out to liberate their land from the Turkish yoke, or would have been capable of doing so.

Of course in times of trouble for the people and crisis for authority, the number of haiduks and haiduk bands would grow, their actions multiply and become more daring. At such times the government orders to stamp out banditry would grow more peremptory, the excuses of local administrators more shrill and heartfelt, and the mood of the people tense. For, unlike the epidemics of ordinary banditry which we retrospectively discover to be forerunners of revolution only because in fact they have preceded it, haiduks were not merely symptoms of unrest but nuclei of potential liberators, recognized by the people as such. If the times were ripe, the 'liberated area' of the Chinese bandits on some mountain of Liang Shan P'o (locus of their 'lair' in the well-known Water Margin novel) would expand to become a region, a province, the nucleus of a force to topple the throne of heaven. The roving bands of outlaws, raiders and Cossacks on the turbulent frontier between state and serfdom on one hand, the open spaces and freedom on the other, would coalesce to inspire and lead the gigantic peasant risings surging upwards along the Volga, headed by a Cossack peoples' pretender, or champion of the true Tsar against the false. Javanese peasants would listen with heightened interest to the story of Ken Angrok, the robber who became the founder of the princely house of Modjopait. If the signs are auspicious, the hundred days during which the maize ripens are past, the time is right, perhaps the millennium of freedom, always latent, always expected, is about to begin. Banditry merges with peasant revolt or revolution. The haiduks,

brilliant in their tunics, formidable in their arms and accoutrements, may be its soldiers.

However, before we can consider the bandit's role in peasant
revolution, we must look at the economic and political factors
which maintain him within the framework of existing society.

# 6

# The Economics and Politics of Banditry

Curious enough, results of a continuous observation and inquiry coincide in this fact: That all bandits are propertyless and they are unemployed. What they may possess is personal and comes only with the success of their reckless adventure.

'*An economic interpretation of the increase of bandits in China*.'[1]

The robber band is outside the social order which fetters the poor, a brotherhood of the free, not a community of the subject. Nevertheless, it cannot opt out of society. Its needs and activities, its very existence, bring it into relations with the ordinary economic, social and political system. This aspect of brigandage is normally neglected by observers, but it is sufficiently important to require a little discussion.

Let us consider first the economics of banditry. Robbers must eat, and supply themselves with arms and ammunition. They must spend the money they rob, or sell their booty. It is true that in the simplest of cases they require very little other than what the local peasantry or herdsman consume – locally produced food, drink and clothing – and may be content if they can get it in ample quantities without the ordinary man's labour. 'Nobody ever refuses them anything,' said a Brazilian landowner. 'It would be stupid to. People give them food, clothes, cigarettes, alcohol. What would they need money for? What would they do with it? Bribe the police, that's all.'[2] However, most bandits we know of live in a monetary economy, even if the surrounding peasantry does not. Where and how do they get their 'coats with the five rows of gold-plated buttons', their guns, pistols and bandoleers, the legendary 'damascene swords with the gilded handle' about which Servian haiduks and Greek *klephtes* bragged, not always with considerable exaggeration?*

*The following is the police inventory of Lampião's equipment (Brazil 1938):

What do they do with the rustled cattle, the travelling merchant's goods? They buy and sell. Indeed, since they normally possess far more cash than ordinary local peasantry, their expenditures may form an important element in the modern sector of the local economy, being redistributed, through local shopkeepers, innkeepers and others, to the commercial middle strata of rural society; all the more effectively redistributed since bandits (unlike the gentry) spend most of their cash locally, and are in any case too proud and too freehanded to

---

*Hat:* leather, of the backwoods type, decorated with six stars of Solomon. Leather chinstrap, 46 cm long, decorated with 50 gold trinkets of miscellaneous origin, to wit: collar and sleeve studs, rectangles engraved with the words Memory, Friendship, Homesickness etc; rings set with various precious stones; a wedding ring with the name Santinha engraved inside. Attached to the front of the hat, a strip of leather 4 by 22 cm with the following ornaments: 2 gold medallions inscribed 'The Lord Be Thy Guide'; 2 gold sovereigns; 1 old Brazilian gold piece with the effigy of the Emperor Pedro II; 2 others, even older, dates respectively 1776 and 1802. At the back of the hat, a strip of leather of equal size, also decorated as follows: 2 gold medallions, 1 small diamond cut in the classic fashion, 4 others of fancy cut.

*Gun:* Brazilian army Mauser, model 1908, no. 314 series B. The bandoleer is decorated with 7 silver crowns of imperial Brazilian coinage and 5 discs of white metal. Safety catch is broken and reinforced with a piece of aluminium.

*Knife:* steel, length 67 cm. The handle is decorated with 3 gold rings. The blade has bullet-marks. Sheath nickle-plated leather, also with bullet-hole.

*Cartridge-pouch:* leather, ornamental. Can contain 121 rounds for Mauser or musket. A whistle is attached by a silver chain. Bullet-hole on left side.

*Haversacks:* 2, copiously embroidered. The embroideries are in vivid colours and done very tastefully. One is closed by means of three buttons, 2 gold, 1 silver; the other has only 1 silver button. On the carrying-straps, 9 buttons in massive silver.

*Neckerchief:* red silk, embroidered.

*Pistol:* Parabellum no. 97, 1918 model, holster, varnished black, very worn.

*Sandals:* one pair, of the same type as habitually worn in the *sertão*, but of excellent quality and finish.

*Tunic:* Blue, with three officer's stripes on the sleeves.

*Blankets:* 2, printed calico, lined with cotton.[3]

Inventory of the possessions of the bandit Lampião drawn up by the police of Bahia, 1938.

bargain. 'The trader sells his goods to Lampião at three times the usual price' it was said in 1930.

All this means that bandits need middlemen, who link them not only to the rest of the local economy but to the larger networks of commerce. Like Pancho Villa, they must have at least one friendly hacienda across the mountain which will take, or arrange to sell, livestock without asking awkward questions. Like the semi-nomads of Tunisia, they may institutionalize arrangements to return stolen cattle against a 'reward', through sedentary middlemen, village innkeepers or dealers who approach the victim to explain, in terms perfectly understood by all concerned, with the news that they know someone who has 'found' the strayed beasts and only wishes their owner to have them back again. Like so many of the Indian dacoit groups, they may raise the money to finance their more ambitious expeditions from moneylenders and traders in their home-base, or even rob some rich caravan virtually on commission for the entrepreneurs who have indicated it to them. For where bandits specialize in robbing transient traffic – as all sensible ones do if they have the luck to live within reach of major routes of trade and communication – they need information about forthcoming shipments or convoys, and they cannot possibly do without some mechanism for selling the loot, which may well consist of commodities for which there is no local demand. Intermediaries are evidently also necessary for kidnappers who demand ransom.

It is therefore a mistake to think of bandits as mere children of nature roasting stags in the greenwood. A successful brigand chief is at least as closely in touch with the market and the wider economic universe as a small landowner or prosperous farmer. Indeed, in economically backward regions his trade may draw him close to that of others who travel, buy and sell. The Balkan cattle- or pig-dealers may well have doubled as bandit leaders, just as merchant captains in pre-industrial days might well dabble in a little piracy (or the other way round), even when not using the good offices of governments to turn themselves into privateers, i.e. legitimate pirates. The history

BRIGAND CHIEF.
PUBLISHED BY W. DAVISON, ALNWICK.—No. 75.

8. Impression of a brigand chief. The brigand image of early
nineteenth-century England owes more to the stage, and perhaps
Robin Hood ballads, than to experience.

of Balkan liberation is familiar with heroic livestock-dealers with a reputation as band-leaders, such as Black George in Serbia or Kolokotrones in Greece; and the history of Balkan banditry is, as we have seen, not unfamiliar with haiduks who put on merchant's garb' for a spell and engage in trade. We tend to be amazed at the transformation of rural toughs in Corsica or inland Sicily into the *Mafiosi* businessmen and entrepreneurs who can recognize the economic opportunities of the international drug-traffic or the construction of luxury hotels as well as the next man, but the cattle-rustling on which so many of them cut their teeth is an activity which widens a peasant's economic horizon. At the very least it tends to put men in touch with those whose horizons are wider than his.

Still, economically speaking the bandit is not a very interesting figure, and though he might well deserve a footnote or two in textbooks of economic development, he probably deserves no more than this. He contributes to the accumulation of local capital – almost certainly in the hands of his parasites rather than in his own free-spending ones. Where he robs transit trade, his economic effect may be analogous to tourist travel, which also extracts income from foreigners: in this sense the brigands of the Sardinian mountains and the developers of the Aga Khan's Costa Smeralda may be economically analogous phenomena.* And that is about all. The real significance of the bandit's economic relationships is therefore different. It lies in the illumination it sheds on his situation within the rural society.

For the crucial fact about the bandit's social situation is its ambiguity. He is an outsider and a rebel, a poor man who refuses to accept the normal roles of poverty, and establishes

* Analogous even in the marginality of their effect on the surrounding economy. For where there is a particularly wide gap between the local economy and the tourist enclaves, much of the income brought in by tourists flows out again to pay for their own consumption of, e.g., luxury motor-boats, champagne and water-skis, which have also to be bought in foreign currency. Just so a brigand chief who robs merchants passing through his region, and buys jewellery, ammunition and conspicuously ornamented swords with the proceeds, or spends these on high living in the capital, is making only a marginal contribution to the income of his region.

his freedom by means of the only resources within reach of the poor, strength, bravery, cunning and determination. This draws him close to the poor: he is one of them. It sets him in opposition to the hierarchy of power, wealth and influence: he is not one of them. Nothing will make a peasant brigand into a 'gentleman', for in the societies in which bandits flourish the nobility and gentry are not recruited from the ranks. At the same time the bandit is, inevitably, drawn into the web of wealth and power, because, unlike other peasants, he acquires wealth and exerts power. He is 'one of us' who is constantly in the process of becoming associated with 'them'. The more successful he is as a bandit, the more he is *both* a representative and champion of the poor *and* a part of the system of the rich.

It is true that the isolation of rural society, the slenderness and intermittency of its relationships, the distances over which they operate, and the general primitivism of rural life, allow the bandit to keep his roles apart with some success. His equivalent in the tightly packed immigrant city slums, the local gangster or political boss (who also, in a sense, stands for the poor against the rich, and sometimes gives to the poor some of his loot from the rich), is much less the rebel and outlaw, much more the boss. His connection with the centres of official wealth and power (e.g. 'City Hall') are much more evident – they may indeed be the most evident thing about him. The rural bandit may be ostensibly quite outside the 'system'. His personal connection with the non-bandit world may be simply that of kinship, of membership in his local village community, that is to say he may apparently belong entirely to the independent sub-world in which peasants live, and into which the gentry, the government, the police, the tax-collectors, the foreign occupiers, only make periodic incursions. Alternatively, as the leader of a free and mobile armed band which depends on nobody, his relations with the centres of wealth and power may appear to be simply those of one sovereign body with others which affect his standing no more than trade negotiations with Britain affect the revolutionary status of Castro's Cuba. And yet, the bandit cannot escape the logic of living in a society of rule and exploitation so easily.

For the basic fact of banditry is that, quite apart from the bandit's need of business contacts, he forms a nucleus of armed strength, and therefore a political force. In the first place, a band is something with which the local system has to come to terms. Where there is no regular or effective machinery for the maintenance of public order – and this is almost by definition the case where banditry flourishes – there is not much point in appealing to the authorities for protection, all the less so as such an appeal will quite likely bring along an expeditionary force of troops, who will lay waste the countryside far more surely than the local bandits:

'I much prefer dealing with bandits than with the police,' said a Brazilian landowner around 1930. 'The police are a bunch of 'dog-killers' who come from the capital with the idea that all the back-woodsmen protect bandits. They think we know all their escape-routes. So their chief object is to get confessions at all costs.... If we say we don't know, they beat us. If we tell them, they still beat us, because that proves that we have been tied up with the bandits.... The backwoodsman can't win.... – And the bandits? – Ah, the bandits behave like bandits. Mind you, you have to know how to handle them so that they don't cause trouble. Still, leaving aside a few of the lads who really are cruel, they cause no harm except when the police is on their tails.'[4]

Isolated estates in such regions have long learned how to establish diplomatic relations with brigands. Ladies of good birth recall in their memoirs how, when still children, they were hustled out of the way as some troop of armed men arrived at the hacienda at nightfall, to be welcomed politely and with offers of hospitality by the head of the house, and to be sent on its mysterious way with equal politeness and assurances of mutual respect. What else could he be expected to do?

Everybody has to come to terms with large and well-established bandits. This means that they are to some extent integrated into established society. The ideal is of course the formal conversion of poachers into gamekeepers, which is by no means uncommon. Cossacks are given land and privileges by lords or tsar, in order to exchange freebooting for the protection of their lord's territory and interests. Gajraj, a chief of the Badhak dacoits, 'risen from the profession of a monkey-showman to be the Robin Hood of Gwalior' in the 1830s, 'had made himself so formidable that the Durbar appointed him to keep the *ghats* or ferries over the Chambal, which he did in a very profitable manner to them.' The Minas, another famous 'robber tribe' in central India, were the terror of Alwar, but in Jaipur they received lands rent-free in return for the duty of escorting convoys of treasure, and were celebrated for their loyalty to the Raja. In India as in Sicily the professions of village and field, or cattle-watchmen, were often interchangeable with that of bandit. The Ramosi, a small dacoit community in Bombay Presidency, were given land, various other perquisites and the right to charge a fee from all travellers in return for guarding the villages. What better safeguard against uncontrolled brigandage than such arrangements?[5]

Whether such arrangements are formalized or not, the inhabitants of bandit-ridden areas often have no other option. Local officials who want to carry out their jobs quietly and without fuss – as which of them do not? – will keep in touch and on reasonable terms with them, or else risk those painful local incidents which give such unwelcome publicity to a district, and cause superior officials to take a poor view of their subordinates. This explains why in really bandit-infested areas campaigns against banditry are so often carried out by special forces brought in from the outside. Local merchants make their own arrangements to safeguard their businesses against constant disruption. Even the locally stationed soldiery and police may merely prefer to keep crime – by tacit or overt agreement with the bandits – below the threshold which will attract the attention of the capital, which leaves plenty of room for banditry, for in the pre-industrial period the eye of central governments does not penetrate too deeply into the undergrowth of rural society, unless its own special interests are involved.

However, not only must local men of wealth or authority come to terms with bandits, but in many rural societies they also have a distinct interest in doing so. The politics of areas ruled by pre-capitalist landowners turn on the rivalries and relationships of the leading landed families and their respective followers and clients. The power and influence of the head of such a family rests, in the last analysis, on the number of men to whom he is patron, offering protection and receiving in turn those services of loyalty and dependence which are the measure of his prestige, and consequently of his capacity to make alliances: fighting, voting or whatever else determines local power. The more backward the area, the more remote, weak or uninterested the higher authorities, the more vital in local politics – or for that matter as regards local influence in national politics – is this capacity of a magnate or gentleman to mobilize 'his' people. If he counts enough swords, guns or votes in the calculus of local politics, he need not even be very rich, as wealth is reckoned in prosperous and economically advanced regions. Of course wealth helps to gain a larger clientele, though only wealth freely, indeed ostentatiously, distributed to demonstrate a nobleman's status and power of patronage. On the other hand a large and formidable following will do more to get a man estates and money than a sound head for figures; though of course the object of such politics is to accumulate not capital but family influence. Indeed, once the pursuit of wealth becomes separable from that of family interest and is superior to it, this kind of politics breaks down.

This is a situation which is ideally suited to banditry. It provides a natural demand and political role for bandits, a local reservoir of uncommitted armed men who, if they can be induced to accept the patronage of some gentleman or magnate, will greatly add to his prestige and may well on a suitable occasion add to his fighting or vote-getting force. (What is more, the establishments of retainers kept by noblemen provide convenient employment for individual bandits, potential or actual.) A wise brigand chief will take care to attach himself only to the dominant local faction, which can guarantee real protection, but even if he does not accept patronage, he can be fairly certain that most local bosses will treat him as a potential ally, and consequently a man to stay on good terms with. This is why in areas remote from effective central authority, like the back country of north-east Brazil until 1940, celebrated bands can flourish for surprisingly long periods: Lampião lasted nearly twenty years. But then Lampião had used such a political situation to build up so strong a force as to constitute not merely a potential reinforcement for any great 'colonel' of the backwoods, but a power in his own right.

In 1926 the Prestes column, a flying guerrilla formation led by a rebellious army officer who was in the process of turning himself into the leader of the Brazilian Communist Party, reached the north-east after two years of mobile operations in other parts of the interior. The Federal Government appealed for help to the Messiah of Juazeiro, Padre Cicero, whose influence had made him the effective political boss of the state of Ceará, partly because a Messiah might help to keep the faithful immune to the social-revolutionary appeals of Prestes and his men. Padre Cicero, who was far from enthusiastic about the presence of federal troops in his fief (he pointed out that his flock was unprepared to oppose anyone whom the government chose to call 'bandits', and the Prestes column did not strike the faithful as anti-social at all), accepted the suggested solution. Lampião was invited to the Father's Jerusalem, the town of Juazeiro, received with all honours, given an official rank as captain by the most senior federal official in residence (an inspector of the ministry of agriculture), together with a rifle and 300 rounds for each of his men, and told to harry the rebels.* The great bandit was immensely excited about this sudden conversion to legitimate status. However, he was advised by a friendly 'colonel' that he was merely making himself a cat's-paw of the government, which would certainly claim, once Prestes had gone, that his commission was invalid, and would equally certainly refuse to honour the promise of

---

*This incident is the foundation for the passage in the romances about Lampião mentioned above.[6]

indemnity for past crimes. This reasoning seems to have convinced Lampião, who promptly gave up his pursuit of Prestes. No doubt he shared the general feeling of all in the backwoods that roving bands of armed men were something one knew how to deal with, but the government was both more incalculable and more dangerous.

The only bandits unable to benefit from so favourable a political situation were those with a reputation for social rebelliousness so marked that any landowner and nobleman would prefer to see them dead. There were never more than a handful of such bands, and their number was kept tiny by the very ease with which peasant bandits could establish relations with men of substance and standing.

Furthermore, the structure of politics in such rural societies provided another, and perhaps an even more formidable reinforcement to banditry. For if the dominant families or faction protected them, the defeated or opposition groups had no recourse except to arms, which meant in extreme cases, to become band-leaders. There are innumerable examples of this. Sleeman in his *Journey through the Kingdom of Oude in 1849–50* gives a list of several, such as Iman Buksh, who still kept up his band and his plundering 'though restored to his estate on his own terms'. The practice was usual, if not inevitable, in Java. A good example of such a situation was that of the department of Cajamarca in Peru in the early twentieth century which produced a number of 'opposition' bandits, notably Eleodoro Benel Zuloeta, against whom some rather elaborate military campaigns were mounted in the middle 1920s.[7] In 1914 Benel, a landowner, had leased the *hacienda* Llaucán, making himself rather unpopular with the local Indian peasantry whose discontent was mobilized against him by the brothers Ramos, who already held the sub-lease of the estate. Benel appealed to the authorities, who massacred the Indians in the usual manner of the times, thus confirming those left in their hostility. The Ramos then felt in a position to finish off Benel, but only managed to kill his son. 'Unfortunately justice failed to act and the crime remained unpunished,' as the historian tactfully puts it, adding that the assassins happened to enjoy the support of some other personal enemies of Benel, e.g. Alvarado of Santa Cruz. Thereupon Benel realized his assets to finance 'a formidable legion of his dependents (*trabajadores*), determined to give their lives in the service of their chief', and moved against Alvarado and the Ramos. This time justice did act, but Benel had fortified his own *hacienda* and defied it. This naturally helped him 'to win further sympathizers whom he supplied with all the necessities of life'.

He was merely the most formidable of a large number of band-leaders who emerged with the virtual breakdown of government authority, in a complex combination of political and personal rivalries, vengeance, political and economic ambition, and social rebellion. As the (military) historian of the campaign puts it:

The peasantry of those settlements was humble and sluggish, incapable of standing up against the little local tyrants. However, to feel alive is to feel rage against injustice. Hence persons of local power and authorities who lacked the intellectual preparation for their difficult duties, managed to unite a now emboldened and determined people against them. . . . The history of all peoples shows that in such situations armed bands are formed. In Chota they went with Benel, in Cutervo with the Vasquez* and others. These men exercised their kind of justice, punishing those who usurped other men's land, formalizing marriages, pursuing criminals and imposing order on the local lords.

At times of elections Congressional Deputies made use of these fighters, supplying them with arms and instructing them to take action against their political adversaries. The armed hosts grew stronger and banditry reached the point at which it caused panic among the peaceful citizenry.[9]

Benel flourished until in 1923 he made the mistake of allying

*The three brothers Vasquez, Avelino, Rosendo and Paulino, were, it seems, smallholders who managed in the course of their activities to become lords of the *haciendas* of Pallac and Camsa. They were tricked into a false 'treaty of peace' and killed at the banquet organized by the sub-prefect to celebrate it.[8]

with some local potentates who planned to overthrow the formidable President Leguía, after which substantial forces were brought into the field and the Cajamarca situation was cleared up, not without considerable efforts. He was finally killed in 1927. The Ramos and Alvarado also disappeared from the scene, together with various other band-leaders.

Such local rivalries are inseparable from banditry. The case of the Clan Macgregor in the sixteenth–eighteenth centuries, and in particular of their most famous member, Rob Roy, is very much in point. For the Macgregors remained a clan of robbers because their enemies left them no other choice but extirpation. (They were indeed formally dissolved and their name forbidden.) Rob Roy's own reputation as a Scottish Robin Hood derives mainly from the fact that he attacked the Duke of Montrose, the successful magnate who had, he felt, done him an injustice. In this way the armed resistance of the 'outs' to the 'ins' of local aristocratic or family politics, may, at least locally and temporarily, satisfy the resentments of the poor against their exploiters, a situation not unknown in other kinds of politics. In any case, where landowning families fight and feud, make and break family alliances, dispute heritages with arms, the stronger accumulating wealth and influence over the broken bones of the weaker, the scope for bands of fighting men led by the disgruntled losers is naturally very large.

The structure of rural politics in the conditions which breed banditry therefore has two effects. On the one hand it fosters, protects and multiplies bandits, on the other it integrates them into the political system. Admittedly both these effects are probably more powerful where the central state apparatus is absent or ineffective and the regional centres of power are balanced or unstable, as in conditions of 'feudal anarchy', in frontier zones, among a shifting mosaic of petty principalities, in the wild back country. A strong emperor, king or even baron establishes his own law on his own lands and hangs freelance bands of armed robbers instead of patronizing them, whether they threaten the social order or merely disrupt trade and disturb property. The British raj scarcely needed to recruit dacoits as escorts for its treasure-transports like the rajas of Jaipur. And men whose power is based on the generation of wealth by wealth, and who do not need (or no longer need) to accumulate wealth by the knife or gun, hire policemen to protect it rather than gangsters. The 'robber barons' of the wild era in American capitalism made the fortunes of the Pinkertons, not of freelance gunmen. It was small and weak business, labour or municipal politics which *had* to negotiate with the mobs, not big business. What is more, with economic development the rich and powerful are increasingly likely to see bandits as threats to property to be stamped out, rather than as one factor among others in the power-game.

Under such circumstances bandits become permanent outcasts, their hand against every 'respectable' man. Perhaps at this stage the anti-mythology of banditry makes its appearance, in which the robber appears as the opposite of the hero, as – to use the terminology of Russian nobles at the end of the eighteenth century – 'a beast in human form', 'ready to pro-

9. 'Sharing the loot'. Note the costumes, the plain with Roman ruins in the background, familiar props of romantic Italian brigand iconography.

'ane all that is holy, to kill, to pillage, to burn, to violate the will of God and the laws of the State'.[10] (It seems certain that, in Russia at least, this myth of the bandit as the negation of humanity arose considerably later than the heroic myth of folk-song and folk-epic.) The mechanism for integrating banditry into normal political life disappears. The robber now belongs only to one part of society, the poor and oppressed. He can either merge with the rebellion of peasant against lord, of traditional society against modernity, of marginal or minority communities against their integration into a wider polity, or with that permanent pendant to the 'straight' or respectable world, the 'bent' or underworld.* But even this now provides less scope for the life of the mountain, the greenwood, and the open highway. Bonnie and Clyde, the heirs of Jesse James, were not typical criminals of the American 1930s, but historical throwbacks. The nearest the really modern strong-arm man gets to the rural life is a barbecue on a country estate gained by urban crime.

* In exceptional cases, as in Sicily and the immigrant ghettoes of the U.S.A., he may also merge with a new bourgeoisie.

# 7
# Bandits and Revolution

Flagellum Dei et commissarius missus a Deo contra usurarios et detinentes pecunias otiosas. (Scourge of God and envoy of God against usurers and the possessors of unproductive wealth.)
*Self-description by Marco Sciarra, Neapolitan brigand chief of the 1590s.*[1]

At this point the bandit has to choose between becoming a criminal or a revolutionary. What if he chooses revolution? As we have seen, social banditry has an affinity for revolution, being a phenomenon of social protest, if not a precursor or potential incubator of revolt. In this it differs sharply from the ordinary underworld of crime, with which we have already had occasion to contrast it. The underworld (as its name implies) is an anti-society, which exists by reversing the values of the 'straight' world – it is, in its own phrase, 'bent' – but is otherwise parasitic on it. A revolutionary world is also a 'straight' world, except perhaps at especially apocalyptic moments when even the anti-social criminals have their access of patriotism or revolutionary exaltation. Hence for the genuine underworld revolutions are little more than unusually good occasions for crime. There is no evidence that the flourishing underworld of Paris provided revolutionary militants or sympathizers in the French revolutions of the eighteenth and nineteenth century though in 1871 the prostitutes were strongly Communard; but as a class they were victims of exploitation rather than criminals. The criminal bandit gangs which infested the French and Rhineland countryside in the 1790s were not revolutionary phenomena, but symptoms of social disorder. The underworld enters the history of revolutions only insofar as the *classes dangereuses* are mixed up with the *classes laborieuses*, mainly in certain quarters of the cities, and because rebels and insurgents are often treated by the authorities as criminals and outlaws but in principle the distinction is clear.

Bandits, on the other hand, share the values and aspirations of the peasant world, and as outlaws and rebels are usually sensitive to its revolutionary surges. As men who have already won their freedom they may normally be contemptuous of the inert and passive mass, but in epochs of revolution this passivity disappears. Large numbers of peasants *become bandits*. In the Ukrainian risings of the sixteenth–seventeenth centuries they would declare themselves Cossacks. In 1860–1 the peasant guerrilla units were formed around, and like, brigand bands: local leaders would find themselves attracting a massive influx of disbanded Bourbon soldiers, deserters, or evaders of military service, escaped prisoners, men who feared persecution for acts of social protest during Garibaldi's liberation, peasants and mountain men seeking freedom, vengeance, loot, or a combination of all these. Like the usual outlaw band, these units would initially tend to form in the neighbourhood of the settlements from which they drew their recruits, establish a base in the near-by mountains or forests, and begin their operations by activities hard to distinguish from those of ordinary bandits. Only the social setting was now different. The minority of the unsubmissive were now joined in mobilization by the majority. In short, to quote a Dutch student of Indonesia, at such times the robber band associates itself with other groups and expresses itself under that guise, whilst the groups which originated with more honest ideals take on the character of bandits'.[2]

An Austrian official in the Turkish service has given an excellent description of the early stages of such a peasant mobilization in Bosnia. At first it only looked like an unusually stubborn dispute about tithes. Then the Christian peasants of Lukovac and other villages gathered, left their houses and went on to the mountain of the Trusina Planina, while those of Gabela and Ravno stopped work and held meetings. While negotiations went on, a band of armed Christians attacked a caravan from Mostar near Nevesinye, killing seven Moslem carters. The Turks thereupon broke off talks. At this point the peasants of Nevesinye all took arms, went on to the mountain and lit alarm-fires. Those of Ravno and Gabela also took arms.

It was evident that a major uprising was about to break out –
in fact the rising which was to initiate the Balkan wars of the
1870s, to detach Bosnia and Hercegovina from the Ottoman
Empire, and to have a variety of important international con-
sequences, which do not concern us here.[3] What does concern
us is the characteristic combination of mass mobilization and
expanded bandit activity in such a peasant revolution.

'Where there is a strong haiduk tradition or powerful independent communities of armed outlaws, free and armed
peasant-raiders, banditry may impose an even more distinct
pattern on such revolts, since it may have already been recognized, in a vague sense, as the relic of ancient or the nucleus of
future freedom. Thus in Saharanpur (Uttar Pradesh, India), the
Gujars, an important minority of the population, had a strong
tradition of independence or 'turbulence' and 'lawlessness' (to
use the phraseology of the British officials). The great Land-
haura estate of the Gujars was broken up in 1813. Eleven years
yater, when times in the countryside were hard, 'the bolder
spirits' in Saharanpur 'sooner than starve, banded themselves
together under a brigand chief named Kallua,' a local Gujar,
and engaged in banditry on either side of the Ganges, robbing
*banias* (the trading and moneylending caste), travellers and
inhabitants of Dehra Dun. 'The motives of the dacoits,' observes
the Gazetteer, 'were perhaps not so much mere plunder as the
desire of the return to the old lawless way of living, unencum-
bered by the regulations of superior authority. In short, the
presence of armed bands implied rebellion rather than mere
law-breaking.'[4]

Kallua, allying with an important *taluqdar** who controlled
forty villages and other disgruntled gentry, soon extended his
revolt by attacking police posts, capturing some treasure from
two hundred police guards and sacking the town of Bhagwan-
pur. Thereupon he declared himself to be the Raja Kalyan
Singh and dispatched messengers in royal fashion to exact
tribute. He now had a thousand men, and announced that he

* Holder of hereditary estates or officer in charge of a *taluq* (district) in
parts of India.

would overthrow the foreign yoke. He was defeated by a force of two hundred Gurkhas, having had 'the incredible presumption to await the attack outside the fort'. The rebellion lasted into the next year ('another hard season ... had given them an accession of new recruits'), and then petered out.

The bandit chief who is regarded as a royal pretender or seeks to legitimize revolution by adopting the formal status of a ruler, is familiar enough. The most formidable examples are perhaps the bandit and Cossack chieftains of Russia, where the great *rasboiniki* always tended to be regarded as miraculous heroes, akin to the champions of the Holy Russian land against the Tatars, if not actually as possible avatars of the 'beggars' tsar' – the good tsar who knew the people and would replace the evil tsar of the *boyars** and the gentry. The great peasant revolt of the seventeenth and eighteenth centuries along the lower Volga were Cossacks – Bulavin, Bolotnikov, Stenka Razin (the hero of folksong) and Yemelyan Pugachov – and Cossacks were in those days communities of free peasant raiders. Like Raja Kalyan Singh, we find them issuing imperial proclamations; like the brigands of southern Italy in the 1860s we find their men killing, burning, pillaging, destroying the written documents which signify serfdom and subjection, but lacking any programme except that of sweeping away the machinery of oppression.

For banditry itself thus to become the revolutionary movement and to dominate it, is unusual. As we have seen (above, pp. 25–6) limitations, both technical and ideological, are such as to make it unsuitable for more than momentary operations of more than a few dozen men, and its internal organization provides no model which can be generalized to be that of an entire society. Even the Cossacks, who developed quite large and structured permanent communities of their own, and very substantial mobilizations for their raiding campaigns, provided only leaders and not models for the great peasant insurrections : it was as 'people's tsars' and not as *atamans*† that they

* Privileged class of high nobles in Russia.
† Elected Cossack chieftains.

mobilized these. Banditry is therefore more likely to come into peasant revolutions as one aspect of a multiple mobilization, and knowing itself to be a subordinate aspect, except in one sense: it provides fighting men and fighting leaders. Before the revolution it may be, to use the phrase of an able historian of Indonesian peasant unrest, 'a crucible out of which emerged a religious revival on one hand, and revolt on the other'.[5] As the revolution breaks out, they may merge with the vast millennial outburst: '*Rampok* bands sprang from the ground like mushrooms, speedily followed by roving groups of the populace, possessed with the expectation of a Mahdi or a millennium.' (This is a description of the Javanese movement after the defeat of the Japanese in 1945.)[6] Yet without the expected Messiah, charismatic leader, 'just king' (or whoever pretends to his crown), or – to continue our Indonesian illustration – the nationalist intellectuals headed by Sukarno who grafted themselves upon this movement, such phenomena are likely to subside, leaving behind them at best rearguard actions by backwoods guerrillas.

Still, when banditry and its companion, millennial exaltation, have reached such a peak of mobilization, the forces which turn revolt into a state-building or society-transforming movement do as often as not appear. In traditional societies accustomed to the rise and fall of political régimes which leave the basic social structure unaffected, gentry, noblemen, even officials and magistrates, may recognize the signs of impending change and consider the time ripe for a judicious transfer of loyalties to what will no doubt turn out to end with a new set of authorities, while expeditionary forces will think of changing sides. A new dynasty may arise, strong in the mandate of heaven, and peaceable men will settle down to their lives again, with hope, doubtless eventually with disillusion, reducing the bandits to the minimum of expected outlawry and sending the prophets back to their hedge-preaching. More rarely, a Messianic leader will appear to build a temporary New Jerusalem. In modern situations, revolutionary movements or organizations will take over. They too may well, after their triumph, find bandit activists drifting back into marginal outlawry, to join the last champions of the old way of life and other 'counter-revolutionaries' in increasingly hopeless resistance.

How indeed do social bandits come to terms with modern revolutionary movements, so remote from the ancient moral world in which they exist? The problem is comparatively easy in the case of national independence movements, since their aspirations can be readily expressed in terms comprehensible to archaic politics, however little they have in common with these in fact. This is why banditry fits into such movements with little trouble: Giuliano turned with equal ease into the hammer of the godless communists and the champion of Sicilian separatism. Primitive movements of tribal or national resistance to conquest may develop the characteristic interplay of bandit guerrillas and populist or millennial sectarianism. In the Caucasus, where the resistance of the great Shamyl to the Russian conquest was based on the development of Muridism among the native Moslem, Muridism and other similar sects were said even in the early twentieth century to provide the celebrated bandit-patriot Zelim Khan (see p. 44 above) with aid, immunity and ideology. He always carried a portrait of Shamyl. In return, two new sects which sprang up among the Ingush mountaineers in that period, one of militants for holy war, the other of unarmed quietists, both equally ecstatic and possibly derived from the Bektashi, regarded Zelim Khan as a saint.[7]

It does not take much sophistication to recognize the conflict between 'our people' and 'foreigners', between the colonized and the colonizers. The peasants of the Hungarian plains who formed the bandit-guerrillas of the famous Sandor Rósza after the defeat of the revolution of 1848–9 may have been moved to rebellion by adventitious acts of the victorious Austrian régime, such as military conscription. (Reluctance to become or remain a soldier is a familiar source of outlaws.) But they were nevertheless 'national bandits', though their interpretation of nationalism might have been very different from the politicians'. The famous Manuel Garcia, 'King of the Cuban countryside', who was reputed single-handed to keep ten thousand soldiers occupied, naturally sent money to the father of Cuban independence, Martí, which the apostle refused, with the habitual dislike of most revolutionaries for criminals. Garcia was killed by treason in 1895, because – so Cuban opinion still holds – he was about to throw in his lot with the revolution.

National liberation bandits are therefore common enough, though commoner in situations where the national liberation movement can be derived from traditional social organization or resistance to foreigners than when it is a novel importation by schoolmasters and journalists. In the mountains of Greece, barely occupied, never effectively administered, the *klephtes* played a larger part in liberation than in Bulgaria, where the conversion to the national cause of eminent haiduks such as Panayot Hitov was notable news. (But then, the Greek mountains were allowed a fair measure of autonomy, through the formations of *armatoles*, technically policing them for the Turkish overlords, in practice doing so only when it suited them. Today's *armatole* captain might be tomorrow's klephtic chief, and the other way round.) What part they play in national liberation is another question.

It is harder for bandits to be integrated into modern movements of social and political revolution which are not primarily against foreigners. Not because they have any more difficulty in understanding, at least in principle, the slogans of liberty, equality and fraternity, of land and freedom, of democracy and communism, if expressed in language with which they are familiar. On the contrary, these are no more than evident truth, the marvel being that men can find the right words for it. 'Truth tickles everyone's nostrils', says Surovkov, the savage Cossack, listening to Isaac Babel reading Lenin's speech from *Pravda*. 'The question is how it's to be pulled from the heap. But he goes and strikes at it straight off, like a hen pecking at a grain.' It is that these evident truths are associated with townsmen, educated men, gentry, with opposition to God and tsar, i.e. with forces normally hostile or incomprehensible to backward peasants.

Still, the junction can be made. The great Pancho Villa was recruited by Madero's men in the Mexican Revolution, and became a formidable general of the revolutionary armies. Perhaps of all professional bandits in the western world, he was the one with the most distinguished revolutionary career. When the emissaries of Madero visited him, he was readily convinced. Madero was a rich and educated man. If he was on the side of the people this proved that he was selfless and the cause therefore untarnished. A man of the people himself, a man of honour, and whose standing in banditry was itself honoured by such an invitation, how could he hesitate to put his men and guns at the disposal of the revolution?[8]

Less eminent bandits may have joined the cause of revolution for very similar reasons. Not because they understood the complexities of democratic, socialist or even anarchist theory (though the last of these contains few complexities), but because the cause of the people and the poor was self-evidently just, and the revolutionaries demonstrated their trustworthiness by unselfishness, self-sacrifice and devotion – in other words by *their personal behaviour*. That is why military service and jail, the places where bandits and modern revolutionaries are most likely to meet in conditions of equality and mutual trust, have seen many political conversions. The annals of modern Sardinian banditry contain several examples. That is also why the men who became the Bourbonist brigand leaders in 1861 were often the same men who had flocked to the standard of Garibaldi, who looked, spoke and acted like a 'true liberator of the people'.

Hence, where the ideological or personal junction between them and the militants of modern revolution can be made, the bandits may join the new-fangled movements as bandits or as individual peasants as they would have joined archaic ones. The Macedonian ones became the fighters of the Komitadji movement (the Internal Macedonian Revolutionary Organization or Imro) in the early twentieth century, and the village schoolmasters who organized them in turn copied the traditional pattern of haiduk-guerrillas in their military structure.

Just as the brigands of Bantam joined the communist rising of 1926, the generality of Javanese followed the secular nationalism of Sukarno or the secular socialism of the Communist Party, the Chinese ones Mao Tse-tung, who was in turn powerfully influenced by the native tradition of popular resistance.

How could China be saved? The young Mao's answer was, 'Imitate the heroes of Liang Shan P'o', i.e. the free bandit-guerrillas of the Water Margin novel.[9] What is more, he systematically recruited them. Were they not fighters, and in their way socially conscious fighters? Did not the 'Red Beards', a formidable organization of horse-thieves which still flourished in Manchuria in the 1920s, forbid its members to attack women, old people and children, but obliged them to attack all civil servants and official personages, but 'if a man has a good reputation we shall leave him one half of his property; if he is corrupt we shall take all his possessions and baggage'? In 1929 the bulk of Mao's Red Army seems to have been composed of such 'declassed elements' (to use his own classification, 'soldiers, bandits, robbers, beggars and prostitutes'). Who was likely to run the risk of joining an outlaw formation in those days except outlaws? 'These people fight most courageously,' Mao had observed a few years earlier. 'When led in a just manner, they can become a revolutionary force.' Did they? We do not know. They certainly gave the young Red Army something of the 'mentality of roving insurgents', though Mao hoped that 'intensified education' might remedy this.

Undoubtedly political consciousness can do much to change the character of bandits. The communist peasant guerrillas of Colombia contain some fighters (but almost certainly not more than a modest minority) who have transferred to them from the former freebooting brigand-guerrillas of the *Violencia*. 'Cuando bandoleaba' (when I was a bandit) is a phrase that may be heard in the conversations and reminiscences that fill so much of a guerrilla's time. The phrase itself indicates the awareness of the difference between a man's past and his present. However probably Mao was too sanguine. Individual bandits may be easily integrated into political units, but collectively, in Colombia at least, they have proved rather un-assimilable into left-wing guerrilla groups.

In any case as bandits their military potential was limited, their political potential even more so, as the brigand wars in southern Italy demonstrate. Their ideal unit was less than twenty men. Haiduk *voivodes* leading more than this were singled out in song and story, and in the Colombian *violencia* after 1948 the very large insurgent units were almost invariably communist rather than grass-roots rebels. Panayot Hitov reports that the *voivode* Ilio, faced with two to three hundred potential recruits, said this was far too many for a single band and they had better form several; he himself chose fifteen. Large forces were, as in Lampião's band, broken up into such sub-units, or temporary coalitions of separate formations. Tactically this made sense, but it indicated a basic incapacity of most grass-roots chiefs to equip and supply large units or to handle bodies of men beyond the direct control of a powerful personality. What is more, each chieftain jealously protected his sovereignty. Even Lampião's most loyal lieutenant, the 'blond devil' Corisco, though remaining sentimentally attached to his old chief, quarrelled with him and took his friends and followers away to form a separate band. The various emissaries and secret agents of the Bourbons who tried to introduce effective discipline and coordination into the brigand movement in the 1860s were as frustrated as all others who have attempted similar operations.

Politically, bandits were, as we have seen, incapable of offering a real alternative to the peasants. Moreover, their traditionally ambiguous position between the men of power and the poor, as men of the people but contemptuous of the weak and the passive, as a force which in normal times operated within the existing social and political structure or on its margins, rather than against it, limited their revolutionary potential. They might dream of a free society of brothers, but the most obvious prospect of a successful bandit revolutionary was to become a landowner, like the gentry. Pancho Villa ended as a *hacendado*,\*

\*Large landowner, owner of estate (*hacienda*).

the natural reward of a Latin American aspirant *caudillo*,\* though no doubt his background and manner made him more popular than the fine-skinned creole aristocrats. And in any case, the heroic and undisciplined robber life did not fit a man much for either the hard, dun-coloured organization-world of the revolutionary fighters or the legality of post-revolutionary life. Few successful bandit-insurgents seem to have played much of a role in Balkan countries they had helped to liberate. Often enough the heroic memories of freedom in the pre-revolutionary mountains, and national insurrection, merely lent an increasingly ironic glitter to strong-arm gangs in the new state, at the disposal of rival political bosses when they did not do a little freelance kidnapping and robbery for their private purposes. Nineteenth-century Greece, nourished on the klephtic mystique, became a gigantic spoils-system, whose prizes were thus competed for. The romantic poets, folklorists and philhellenes had given the highland brigands a European reputation. M. Edmond About, in the 1850s, was more struck by the shoddy reality of the 'Roi des Montagnes' than by the highflown phrases of klephtic glory.

The bandits' contribution to modern revolutions was thus ambiguous, doubtful and short. That was their tragedy. As bandits they could at best, like Moses, discern the promised land. They could not reach it. The Algerian war of liberation began, characteristically enough, in the wild mountains of the Aurès, traditional brigand territory, but it was the very unbandit-like Army of National Liberation which finally won independence. The Chinese Red Army soon ceased to be a bandit-like formation. More than this. The Mexican Revolution contained two major peasant components: the typical bandit-based movement of Pancho Villa in the north, the entirely unbandit-like agrarian agitation of Zapata in Morelos. In military terms, Villa played an immeasurably more important part on the national scene, but neither the shape of Mexico nor even of Villa's own north-west was changed by it. Zapata's

---

\* Military chieftain establishing political power, a sadly familiar figure in Latin American history.

ovement was entirely regional, its leader was killed in 1919,
s military forces were of no great consequence. Yet this was
ae movement which injected the element of agrarian reform
ato the Mexican Revolution. The brigands produced a poten-
al *caudillo* and a legend – not least, a legend of the only
Mexican leader who tried to invade the land of the *gringos* in
ais century.* The peasant movement of Morelos produced a
ocial revolution; one of the three which deserve the name in
ae history of Latin America.

* The most dramatic evidence of this comes from the village of San José
e Gracia in the uplands of Michoacan, Mexico, which – like so many
Mexican villages – expressed its popular aspirations by mobilizing under the
anner of Christ the King *against* the revolution (as part of the *Cristero*
aovement, best known through Graham Greene's *The Power and the
Glory*). Its excellent historian points out that it naturally 'abhorred the
reat figures of the Revolution' with two exceptions: President Cardenas
(1934–40) for distributing the land and ending the persecution of religion
ad – Pancho Villa. 'These have become popular idols.'[10] Even in 1971 the
eneral store in a very similar township of the same area, a place not visibly
auch given to literature, contained *The Memoirs of Pancho Villa*.

# 8

# The Expropriators

Finally we must glance at what may be called 'quasi-banditry', that is to say at revolutionaries who do not themselves belong to the original world of Robin Hood, but who in one way or another adopt his methods and perhaps even his myth. The reasons for this may be partly ideological, as among the Bakuninist anarchists who idealized the bandit as

the genuine and sole revolutionary – a revolutionary without fine phrases, without learned rhetoric, irreconcilable, indefatigable and indomitable, a popular and social revolutionary, non-political and independent of any estate (Bakunin).

They may be a reflection of the immaturity of revolutionaries who, though their ideologies are new, are steeped in the traditions of an ancient world, like the Andalusian anarchist guerrillas after the Civil War of 1936–9 who fell naturally into the ways of the old 'noble bandoleros', or the German journeymen of the early nineteenth century, who – equally naturally – called their secret revolutionary brotherhood, which eventually became Karl Marx's Communist League, the League of the Outlaws. (The Christian-communist tailor Weitling actually at one stage planned a revolutionary war waged by an army of outlaws.) Or else the reasons may be technical, as in guerrilla movements which are obliged to follow substantially similar tactics as social bandits, and on the cloak-and-dagger fringe of illegal revolutionary movements where the smugglers, terrorists, forgers, spies and 'expropriators' operate. In this chapter we shall deal primarily with 'expropriation', the long-established and tactful name for robberies designed to supply revolutionaries with funds.

The history of this tactic remains to be written. Probably it appeared at the point where the libertarian and authoritarian lines of the modern revolutionary movement, the *sans-culotte* and the Jacobins, crossed: by Blanqui out of Bakunin. The place of birth was almost certainly the anarchist-cum-terrorist milieu of tsarist Russia in the 1860s and 1870s. The bomb, which was the standard equipment of Russian expropriators in the early twentieth century, points to their terrorist derivation. (In the Western tradition of bank-robbery, whether political or ideologically neutral, the gun has always prevailed.) The term 'expropriation' itself was originally not so much a euphemism for hold-up jobs, as a reflection on a characteristically anarchist confusion between riot and revolt, between crime and revolution, which regarded not only the gangster as a truly libertarian insurrectionary, but such simple activities as looting as a step towards the spontaneous expropriation of the bourgeoisie by the oppressed. We need not blame serious anarchists for the excesses of the lunatic fringe of declassed intellectuals which indulged in such fancies. Even among them 'expropriation' gradually settled down as a technical term for robbing money for the good of the cause, normally – and significantly – from those symbols of the impersonal power of money, the banks.

Ironically enough it was not so much the local and scattered forms of direct action by anarchists or *narodnik*\* terrorists which made 'expropriation' a public scandal in the international revolutionary movement, as the activities of the Bolsheviks during and after the 1905 revolution; and more particularly the famous Tiflis (Tbilisi) hold-up of 1907, which netted the party over 200,000 roubles, unfortunately mainly in large and readily traced denominations which got the devoted exiles like Litvinov (subsequently Commissar for Foreign Affairs of the U.S.S.R.) and L. B. Krassin (subsequently in charge of Soviet foreign trade) into trouble with Western policemen, when they tried to change them. It was a good stick with which to beat Lenin, always suspect to other Russian sectors of social democracy for his alleged 'Blanquist' tendencies, just as later it was a good stick with which to beat Stalin, who, as a leading

---

\* Member of the Russian populist revolutionary movements in the later nineteenth century.

Bolshevik in Transcaucasia, was deeply involved in it. The accusations were unfair. Lenin's Bolsheviks differed from other social democrats merely in not condemning any form of revolutionary activity, including 'expropriations' *a priori*; or rather, in lacking the cant which officially condemned operations which, as we now know, not only illegal revolutionaries but also governments of all complexions practise whenever they think them essential. Lenin did his best to fence off 'expropriations' from ordinary crime and unorganized freebooting with an elaborate system of defences: they were to be conducted only under organized party auspices, and in a framework of socialist ideology and education, in order not to degenerate into crime and 'prostitution'; they were to be undertaken only against state property, etc. Stalin, though no doubt he went into these activities with his usual lack of humanitarian scruple, was doing no more than applying party policy. Indeed, the 'expropriations' in turbulent and gun-happy Transcaucasia were neither the largest – the record was probably held by the Moscow hold-up of 1906, which netted 875,000 roubles – nor the most frequent. If anything Latvia, in which the Bolshevik papers publicly acknowledged at least some of the income from expropriations (as socialist journals usually record donations), was most given to this form of selfless robbery.

The study of the Bolshevik 'expropriations' is therefore not the best way to grasp the nature of such quasi-bandit activity, and this writer knows too little about the most prominent expropriations of the 1960s, those undertaken by various forms of revolutionaries in parts of Latin America to say anything of interest about them. All that the hold-ups of official Marxists demonstrate is the obvious fact that such activities tend to attract a certain type of militant, the sort of man who, though often longing for the really high-status work such as drafting theoretical statements and addressing Congress, feels happier with a gun and a lot of presence of mind. The late 'Kamo (Semyon Arzhakovich Ter-Petrossian, 1882–1922), a remarkably brave and tough Armenian terrorist who threw in his lot with the Bolsheviks, was a splendid example of such a political

gun-fighter. He was the chief organizer of the Tiflis expropriation, though as a matter of principle never spending more than
fifty copecks a day on his personal needs. The end of the civil
war left him free to realize his long-cherished ambition to edu-
cate himself properly in Marxist theory, but after a brief in-
terval he yearned once again for the excitements of direct
action. He was probably lucky to die in a bicycle accident when
he did. Neither his age nor the atmosphere of the Soviet Union
in subsequent years would have been congenial to his type of
Old Bolshevism.

The best way to bring the phenomenon of 'expropriation' before readers who have no great acquaintance with ideological
gun-fighters, is to sketch the portrait of one of them. I choose
the case of Francisco Sabaté Llopart (1913–60), one of the
group of anarchist guerrillas who raided Catalonia from bases
in France after the Second World War, and almost all of whom
are now dead or in jail: the Sabaté brothers, José Luis
Facerias, the waiter from the Barrio Chino in Barcelona (probably the ablest and most intelligent), Ramon Capdevila, named
'Burntface' or 'Caraquemada', the boxer (probably the toughest,
and one of the longest-lived – he lasted until 1963), Jaime Pares
'El Abissinio', the factory operative José Lopez Penedo, Julio
Rodriguez 'El Cubano', Paco Martinez, Santiago Amir Gruana
'El Sheriff', Pedro Adrover Font 'El Yayo', the young and
always hungry José Pedrez Pedrero 'Tragapanes', Victor Es-
pallargas whose pacifist principles allowed him to take part
in bank-raids but only unarmed, and all the others whose names
now live only in police records and the memories of their
families and a few anarchist militants.

Barcelona, that hill-compressed, hard-edged, and passionate
capital of proletarian insurrection, was their *maquis*, though
they knew enough about the mountains to make their way there
and back. Commandeered taxis and stolen cars were their
transport, bus-queues or the gates of football stadia their rendezvous. Their accoutrements were the raincoat so dear to
urban gunmen from Dublin to the Mediterranean, and the
shopping bag or briefcase to hide guns or bombs. 'The idea' of

anarchism was their motive: that totally uncompromising and lunatic dream which a great many of us share, but which few except Spaniards have ever tried to act upon, at the cost of total defeat and impotence for their labour movement. Theirs was the world in which men are governed by pure morality as dictated by conscience; where there is no poverty, no government, no jails, no policemen, no compulsion and discipline except that of the inner light; no social bond except fraternity and love; no lies; no property; no bureaucracy. In this world men are pure like Sabaté, who never smoked or drank (except, of course, a little wine with meals) and ate like a shepherd even when he had just robbed a bank. In this world reason and enlightenment bring men out of darkness. Nothing stands between us and this ideal except the forces of the devil, bourgeois, fascists, Stalinists, even backsliding anarchists, forces which must be swept away, though of course without our falling into the diabolical pitfalls of discipline and bureaucracy. It is a world in which the moralists are also gunfighters, both because guns kill enemies and because they are the means of expression of men who cannot write the pamphlets or make the great speeches of which they dream. Propaganda by action replaces that by word.

Francisco Sabaté Llopart 'Quico' discovered 'the idea', in common with an entire generation of Barcelona working-class youths aged between thirteen and eighteen, in the great moral awakening which followed the proclamation of the Spanish Republic in 1931. He was one of five children of an unpolitical municipal watchman in Hospitalet de Llobregat, just outside Barcelona, and became a plumber. Except for Juan, a highly strung boy who wanted to become a priest, the boys looked to the left, following Pepe the fitter, the eldest of the family. Three of them are now dead. Francisco himself was not a great man for books, though later he was to make heroic efforts to read, in order to be able to discuss Rousseau, Herbert Spencer and Bakunin as a good anarchist should, and took even greater pride in his two daughters at the lycée in Toulouse, who merely read *Express* and *France-Observateur*. He was not semi-literate, and the Franco accusation that he was rankled bitterly.

He was seventeen when he joined the libertarian youth organization, and began to absorb the marvellous truth in the libertarian Athenaeums in which the young militants met for education and inspiration; for to be politically conscious in those days in Barcelona meant to become an anarchist as certainly as in Aberavon it meant to join the Labour Party. But no man can escape his fate. Sabaté was designed by nature for his subsequent career. Just as there are some women who are only fully themselves in bed, so there are men who only realize themselves in action. Big-jawed, thick-browed, looking smaller than his size because of his stockiness – though he was actually a little less muscular than he appeared – Sabaté was one of these. In repose he was nervous and awkward. He could barely sit in comfort in an armchair, let alone in a café in which, like a good gunfighter, he automatically chose the seat with cover, a view of the door and in reach of the back exit. As soon as he stood with a gun on a street-corner he became relaxed, and in a gruff way, radiant. 'Muy sereno' his comrades described him at such moments, sure of his reflexes and instincts, those hunches which can be perfected but not created by experience; sure above all of his courage and his luck. No man without remarkable natural aptitudes would have lasted nearly twenty-two years of unbroken outlawry, interrupted only by jail.

It seems that almost from the start he found himself in the *grupos especificos* or action groups of young libertarians, which fought duels with the police, assassinated reactionaries, rescued prisoners and expropriated banks for the purpose of financing some small journal, the distaste of anarchists for organization making regular fund-raising difficult. His activities were local. In 1936, by that time married – or rather demonstratively *not* married – to a servant-girl from Valencia, whose character had the same classic simplicity as his, he was still merely a member of the revolutionary committee in Hospitalet. He went to the front of the *Los Aguiluchos* (the 'Young Eagles') column, commanded by Garcia Oliver, as a centurion, responsible as the name implies, for a centuria of a hundred men. As his gifts for orthodox leadership were clearly small, he was soon side-tracked into an armourer's job, for which his familiarity with guns and explosives fitted him. Also, he had a natural bent for machinery, as for combat. He was the kind of man who builds himself a motorbike from scrap. He never became an officer.

Sabaté fought quietly with his column (later merged into the 28th Ascaso Division, commanded by Gregorio Jover) until the battle of Teruel. He was not used for the special guerrilla units of the army, which suggests that his gifts were unrecognized. Then, during the battle, he deserted. The official explanation is that he quarrelled with the communists, which is more than likely. He returned to lead a clandestine existence in Barcelona, and for practical purposes he never abandoned it for the rest of his life.

His first activity in Barcelona against the 'Stalino-bourgeois coalition' was to liberate a comrade wounded in a brush with the (Republican) police; his second, still under orders from the anarchist Youth Committee of Defence, to liberate four men imprisoned after the rising of May 1937, who were being trans-ported between those two poles of the anarchist militant's globe, the Model Prison and the Fortress of Montjuich. Then he was himself imprisoned in Montjuich and tried to escape. His wife smuggled a gun to him in his next jail at Vich and he fought his way out. By now he was a marked man. His comrades therefore found a cover for him by sending him to the front with another anarchist unit, the 26th Durruti Division, with which he stayed to the end. It should perhaps be added for the benefit of non-anarchist readers that Sabaté's attachment to the Republican cause and hatred of Franco never wavered throughout these surprising proceedings.

The war ended. After the usual spell in a French concentra-tion camp, Sabaté found himself working as a fitter near An-goulême. (His brother Pepe, an officer, had been caught and jailed in Valencia; young Manolo was barely twelve years old.) There the German occupation caught him, and soon pushed him back into clandestinity. But unlike many other Spanish refugees, his resistance activities were marginal. Spain, and only Spain was his passion. Around 1942 he was back on the Pyrenean border, ill but already anxious to raid. From this time he began to operate on his own, reconnoitring the frontier.

At first he went round the mountain farms as a travelling mechanic and general mender-of-things. Then, for a while, he joined a group of smugglers. Subsequently he established two bases for himself, settling as a small farmer in one of them, the Mas Casenobe Loubette near Coustouges, within sight of Spain. The frontier between La Preste and Ceret was to remain 'his' beat ever after. There he knew the routes and the people and had his bases and depots. This eventually doomed him, for it defined the area within which the police could expect him to be within a few kilometres. On the other hand it was inevitable. Efficient organizations can route couriers or guerrillas anywhere between Irun and Port Bau. A congeries of small craft enterprises, like the anarchist underground, is one of local men who are in darkness outside the small area they have themselves prospected. Sabaté knew his sector of the mountains. He knew the routes thence to Barcelona. Above all, he knew Barcelona. These were his 'manor'. There and nowhere else in Spain did he operate.

He seems not to have raided before the spring of 1945, though he did some guiding and perhaps liaison work. In May of that year he began to make a name for the rescue of a comrade from the police in the middle of Barcelona. And then came the events which made him a hero. One of his guerrilla parties attracted the attention of the Civil Guard in Bañolas, his dispersal point after crossing the mountains. The police flourished their arms – Sabaté was punctilious about not shooting until the other side made a move to draw – and one was killed, the other disarmed. He by-passed the hue-and-cry by the simple method of walking in easy stages to Barcelona. By the time he arrived the police was informed. He walked straight into an ambush at the habitual meeting place of the comrades, a milk-bar in the Calle Santa Teresa. Sabaté's hunch for ambushes was extraordinary. The four labourers coming slowly towards him chatting were, it was clear to him, policemen. He therefore continued slowly and carelessly walking *towards* them. At about thirty feet he reached for his sub-machine gun and took aim.

The war between police and terrorists is one of nerves as well as of guns. Whoever is more frightened has lost the initiative. The key to Sabaté's unique career after 1945 lay in the moral superiority he established over the police by the conscious policy of always, when possible, advancing *towards* them. The four plain-clothes men were unnerved, made for cover, and opened a rather ragged fire while he got away. He did not shoot.

It was a sign of his relative inexperience that he now went home, to arrange for a meeting with his brother Pepe, who had just come out of prison in Valencia. The house was already watched, but Sabaté only went in for a moment to leave a note, and immediately left by the back to sleep in the woods. This seems to have taken the police by surprise. When he returned next morning he smelled the ambush, but it was too late. His route was already barred by a couple of obvious police-wagons. He strolled carelessly past them. What he did not know was, that one of the wagons contained two captured anarchists who were to identify him. They did not. Sabaté strolled casually on to safety.

The hero needs bravery for his role, and he had proved it. He needs guile and perspicacity. He needs luck, or in mythical terms, invulnerability. Surely, the man who smelled and escaped ambushes had proved these. But he also needs victory. He had not yet proved this – except by killing policemen – and by rational standards could never prove it. But by the standards of the poor, oppressed and ignorant men whose horizons are bounded by their *barrio** or at most their city, the mere capacity for the outlaw to survive against the concentrated forces of the rich and their jailers and policemen is victory enough. And henceforth nobody in Barcelona, a city which breeds more

*City quarter or district.

ompetent judges of good rebels than most, could doubt that
abaté possessed this capacity. Least of all himself.

The years 1944 to the early 1950s saw a systematic attempt to
verthrow Franco by private invasions across the frontier from
'rance, but more seriously, by guerrilla action. This episode is
ot widely known, though the attempts were serious enough.
Official communist sources list a total of 5,371 actions by
uerrillas in the period between 1944 and 1949, with a peak of
,317 in 1947, and Franco sources estimate guerrilla casualties
f 400 in the largest *maquis*, in southern Aragon.[1] Though
uerrillas operated in virtually all mountain areas, especially
n the north and in southern Aragon, the Catalan guerrillas,
vho were almost wholly anarchist, unlike the others, were of no
nilitary significance. They were too poorly organized and un-
lisciplined, and their objectives were those of their cadres,
nen with parish-pump perspectives. It was among such anar-
hist groups that Sabaté now operated.

Considerations of high politics, strategy and tactics, hardly
ffected men of his kind. For them such things were always
hadowy unrealities, except insofar as they were vivid because
ymbolic of immorality. Theirs was an abstract world in which
ree men with guns stood on one side, policemen and jails on
he other, typifying the human condition. Between them
rouched the mass of undecided workers who would one day
- perhaps tomorrow? – rise in majestic power, inspired by the
xample of morality and heroism. Sabaté and his friends found
olitical rationalizations for their exploits. He put bombs into
ome Latin American consulates as a protest against a U.N.
ote. He fired leaflets out of a home-made bazooka over the
ootball crowds to make propaganda, and held up bars to
lay anti-Franco speeches on tape-recorders. He robbed banks
or the cause. Yet those who knew him agree that what really
ounted for him was the example of action rather than its effect.
What moved him, irresistibly and obsessively, was the desire to
;o raiding in Spain, and the eternal duel between the militants
nd the State: the plight of imprisoned comrades, the hatred
f policemen. An outsider may wonder why none of the groups

ever made a serious attempt to assassinate Franco or even th
Captain-General of Catalonia, but only Signor Quintela of th
Barcelona police. But Quintela was head of the 'Social Brigade
He had, it was said, tortured comrades with his own hands. I
is highly typical, not least of anarchist disorganization, tha
when Sabaté planned to assassinate him he found another grou
of activists already independently on the same trail.

From 1945 on, therefore, the heroic exploits and demonstra
tions multiplied. The official record (not altogether reliable
credits Sabaté with five attacks in 1947, one in 1948, and no les
than fifteen in 1949, the year of the Barcelona guerrillas' glor
and disaster. That January the Sabatés took charge of the jol
of raising funds for the defence of some prisoners, a list o
whom a certain Ballester had brought out of jail together witl
a police tail. In February Pepe Sabaté shot a policeman wh
was ambushing the brothers at their rendezvous in the doorway
of the Ciné Condal, by the Paralelo. Shortly after this the polic
surprised Pepe and José Lopez Penedo asleep in La Torrasa, a
suburb of flamenco-singing southern immigrants, and they
fought a gun-battle in their underwear between the front doo
and the dining-room. Lopez died; Pepe, badly wounded, es
caped almost naked, swam the river Llobregat, held up a passer
by for clothes, and walked five miles to a safe refuge where he
was joined by his brother, who got him a doctor and saw to
his transport to France.

In March Sabaté and the Los Manos group of young
Aragonese joined up to kill Quintela, but only killed a couple
of lesser Falangists by mistake. (Someone had issued a genera
threat to attack the police headquarters, which frightened the
police, but also warned them.) In May Sabaté and Faceria
joined forces to put their bombs into the Brazilian, Peruvian
and Bolivian consulates, Sabaté calmly dismantling one after
the alarm had been given so as to exchange the time mechanism
for immediate detonation. Other bombs he placed with the
simple help of a fishing-rod. By the autumn, however, the police
had the situation under control. In October Pepe fell in ambush
having just fought his way out of another over the dead body

of a policeman. That month saw the end of the bulk of the fighting men.

In December a third of the Sabaté brothers went. Young Manolo had never been a man of 'the idea'. His ambition was to be a *torero*, and he had left home in his teens to follow the *novilladas** in Andalusia, but the adventure represented by his brothers was equally tempting. They did not let him join them, preferring him to study and better himself, but the Sabaté name got him into the group of the redoubtable Ramon Capdevila ('Caraquemada' or 'Burntface'), an ex-boxer who had abandoned the ring on getting 'the idea' and was now a considerable expert in explosives. One of the few guerrillas whose activities made some sense, he raided in the provinces, blowing up pylons and suchlike. Inexperienced, Manolo lost his way in the hills after a brush with the police, and was arrested. The Sabaté name guaranteed his execution. He was shot in 1950, leaving behind nothing but a French watch.

By this time, however, Sabaté was no longer in Spain. Troubles, mainly with the French police, were to keep him away for nearly six years. They had begun in 1948 when he was stopped by a gendarme on one of his innumerable trips to the frontier in a hired car (Sabaté always liked transport which allowed him to keep his hands free.) He had lost his head, broken and run. They had found his gun, and later a sizeable collection of equipment, explosives, radios, etc. in his farm at Coustouges. In November he was sentenced *in absentia* to three years in jail and a fine of 50,000 francs. On advice, he appealed and in June 1949 got a harmless two months, which was later raised to six, with five years' *interdiction de séjour*. Henceforth his visits to the frontier were to be illegal even from the French side, and he lived under police supervision far from the Pyrenees.

In fact, he did not get out of jail for a year, for the French police tied him to another and much more serious affair, a hold-up at the Rhone-Poulenc factory in May 1948, as a result

---

* Bullfights for junior bulls and fighters.

of which a watchman had died. It is characteristic of the staggering unrealism of the activists, whose very existence depended on the benevolent blindness of the French authorities, that they expropriated the bourgeoisie for the good of the cause with as much readiness in Lyons as in Barcelona. (Only the intelligent Facerias avoided this; *he* robbed his non-Spanish banks in Italy.) It is equally typical that they left a back-trail as visible as a landing-strip. Thanks to some very good lawyers, the case against Sabaté was never quite proved; though the police had at one point lost patience and actually extracted a confession from him after beating him up for several days, or so his lawyer claimed, not without plausibility. After four *non-lieus* the case was still pending at the time of his death. However, in addition to considerable worry, the affair cost him the best part of another two years in jail.

When Sabaté got his head at least temporarily above these rough waters, he found the political situation utterly changed. In the early 1950s all parties abandoned guerrilla warfare for more realistic tactics. The militants were therefore alone.

It was a desperate blow. Sabaté, though quite incapable of obeying any instructions with which he disagreed, was a loyal man. Not to have the approval of the comrades hurt him almost physically, and until his death he made constant but unavailing efforts to regain it. The blow was not softened by an offer to settle him in Latin America. As well offer Othello a consular post in Paris instead of an army. And so, in April 1955 he was back in Barcelona. Early in 1956 he teamed up with Facerias for a joint operation – the two individualists soon split up – and stayed for several months, publishing a small journal, *El Combate,* and holding up the Banco Central two-handed with the aid of a dummy bomb. In November he was back again for a hold-up of the large textile firm Cubiertos y Tejados, which netted almost a million pesetas.

After that the French police, tipped off by the Spaniards, caught up with him again. He lost his base in La Preste, and was once again imprisoned. He got out of jail in May 1958, but was ill for the next few months after a bad operation for ulcers. Facerias had been killed meanwhile. Then he began to plan his next and last raid.

By this time he was alone, except for a few friends. Even the organization, by its silent disapproval, seemed to lend colour to the fascists and bourgeois who thought of him as a mere bandit. Even his friends told him, with complete accuracy, that another raid would be suicidal. He had aged notably. All he had left was his reputation as a hero and the passionate conviction which lent this otherwise not very articulate man a remarkable power to persuade. This he carried round the *émigré* meetings of France in defiance of police regulations, a stocky figure with a bulging brief-case who shied away from sitting in corners. He was *not* a bandit. The cause could *not* be left without champions in Spain. Who knows, perhaps he would be the Fidel Castro of his country? Could they not understand?

He got together a little money and talked a fair number of men, mostly inexperienced, into taking arms. He went with the first group, consisting of Antonio Miracle, a bank clerk relatively fresh from clandestinity, two youngsters of barely twenty, Rogelio Madrigal Torres and Martin Ruiz, and an otherwise unknown married man of thirty, a certain Conesa; all from Lyons and Clermont-Ferrand. The rest never made the journey. He saw his family again at the end of 1959, but without telling them his plans. And then he went to what all, except perhaps himself, knew to be death.

It can at least be said that he died as he would have wished to. The group was picked up by the police within a few miles of the frontier, doubtless on a tip-off. They broke away. Two days later they were surrounded in a lonely farm and besieged for twelve hours. After the setting of the moon Sabaté stampeded the cattle with a hand-grenade and crept silently away after killing his last policeman; but wounded. All his companions were killed. Two days later, on January 6th, he held up the 5.20 train from Gerona to Barcelona at the small stop of Fornells and ordered the driver to go straight through. It was impossible, for at Massanet-Massanas all trains switch to electric traction. By this time Sabaté's foot-wound had turned

septic. He limped, had a high fever, and kept himself going
with morphine injections from his first-aid kit. The other two
wounds, a graze behind the ear and an entry-and-exit wound in
the shoulder, were less serious. He ate the engine-crew's break
fast.

At Massanet he slipped back into the post-van, climbed on
the new electric engine and worked his way forward to the
driver's cabin. He held up the new crew. They also told him
that it was impossible, short of risking accidents, to drive
straight to Barcelona in defiance of the timetable. At this stage I
think he knew that he would die.

Shortly before the small town of San Celoni he made them
slow down and jumped off. By this time the police had been
alerted all along the line. He asked a carter for wine, for his
fever made him thirsty, and drank it in great gulps. Then he
asked an old woman for a doctor. She directed him to the other
end of town. It seems he mistook the house of the doctor's
servant – the surgery was empty – and knocked up a certain
Francisco Berenguer, who was clearly suspicious of the hag
gard, unwashed figure in a boiler-suit with pistol and sub
machine gun, and refused to let him in. They struggled. Two
policemen appeared at the ends of the two streets at whose
corner the two men wrestled. Sabaté bit Berenguer's hand to
get at his pistol – he could no longer get at the sten-gun – and
wounded one last policeman before he fell at the corner of the
Calle San José and San Tecla.

'If he had not been wounded,' they say in San Celoni, 'they
would not have got him; for the police were afraid.' But the
best epitaph is that of one of his friends, a brick-layer in Per
pignan, spoken before the Maillol Venus which graces that
civilized town's centre. 'When we were young, and the Republic
was founded, we were knightly though also spiritual (*cabal
leresco pero espiritual*). We have grown older, but not Sabaté
He was a *guerillero* by instinct. Yes, he was one of those
Quixotes who come out of Spain.' It was said, and perhaps
rightly, without irony.

But better than any formal epitaph, he received the final ac-

blade of the bandit-hero, the champion of the oppressed, which
the refusal to believe in his death. 'They say', said a taxi-
driver a few months after his end, 'that they fetched his father
and sister to look at the body, and they looked at it and said:
"it is not he, it is someone else".' 'They' were wrong in fact,
but right in spirit, for he was the sort of man who deserved the
legend. More: whose only possible reward could be heroic
legend. By any rational and realistic standards his career was a
waste of life. He never achieved anything, and indeed even the
proceeds of his robberies were increasingly swallowed up by the
spiralling costs of semi-private clandestinity – false papers,
arms, bribes, etc. – so that little was left for propaganda. He
never even looked like achieving anything except a death-
sentence for anyone known to be associated with him. The
theoretical justification of the insurrectionary, that the sheer
will to make a revolution can catalyse the objective conditions
for revolution, could not apply to him, since what he and his
comrades did could not conceivably have produced a larger
movement. Their own argument, simpler and more Homeric,
that since men are good, brave and pure by nature, the mere
sight of devotion and courage, repeated often enough, must
shame them out of their torpor, had equally little chance of
success. It could only produce legend.

By his purity and simplicity Sabaté was fitted to become a
legend. He lived and died poor; until the end the wife of the
celebrated bank-robber worked as a servant. He robbed banks
not simply for money, but as a *torero* fights bulls, to demonstrate courage. Not for him the discovery of the astute Facerias,
that the safest way of collecting money is to raid a certain kind
of hotel at 2 a.m., certain that the solid bourgeois found there
in bed with a variety of mistresses would give up his cash wil-
lingly and not talk to the police.* To take money without expos-
ing oneself to risk, was unmanly – Sabaté always preferred to
knock over a bank with fewer people than were technically
required, for this reason – and conversely, to take money at the

* Actually, Spanishness defeated even this plan; one wealthy lover, perhaps anxious to impress his youthful girl-friend, resisted and was killed.

risk of one's own life was, in some moral sense, to *pay* for i
To walk always *towards* the police was not only a sour
psychological tactic, but the hero's way. He could no doul
have forced the engine-crews of his train to drive throug
though it might not have done him much good; but he cou
not, morally, risk the lives of men who did not fight him.

To become a public legend a man must have simple outline
To be a tragic hero everything about him must be pared awa
leaving him silhouetted against the horizon in the quintesser
tial posture of his role, as Don Quixote is against his windmill
and the gunfighters of the mythical West are, solitary in th
white sunlight of their empty midday streets. That is ho
Francisco Sabaté Llopart stood. It is just that he should be s
remembered, in the company of other heroes.

# The Bandit as Symbol

We have so far looked at the reality of social bandits, and at their legend or myth chiefly as a source of information about that reality, or about the social roles bandits are supposed to play (and therefore often do), the values they are supposed to represent, their ideal – and therefore often also real – relationship with the people. Yet such legends operate not simply among those familiar with a particular bandit, or any bandits, but very much more widely and generally. The bandit is not only a man, but a symbol. In concluding this study of banditry, we must therefore also look at these remoter aspects of our subject. They are curious in at least two ways.

The bandit legend among the peasants themselves is peculiar, because the immense personal prestige of celebrated outlaws does not prevent their fame from being rather short-lived. As in so many other respects, Robin Hood, though in most ways the quintessence of bandit legend, is also rather untypical. No real original Robin Hood has ever been identified beyond dispute, whereas all other bandit-heroes I have been able to check, however mythologized, can be traced back to some identifiable individual in some identifiable locality. If Robin Hood existed, he flourished before the fourteenth century, when the cycle is first recorded in writing. His legend has therefore been popular for a minimum of six hundred years. All other bandit-heroes mentioned in this book (with the exception of the protagonists of the Chinese popular novels) are much more recent. Stenka Razin, the insurgent leader of the Russian poor, dates back to the 1670s, but the bulk of such figures whose legends were alive in the nineteenth century, when such ballads were systematically collected, only date back to the eighteenth – which therefore appears to be the golden age of bandit-heroes: Janošik in Slovakia, Diego Corrientes in Andalusia, Mandrin in France, Rob Roy in Scotland, for that

10. The ritual of public execution belongs to the myth of urban crime rather than to social banditry. Here the distinction between Hood and Turpin, Mandrin and Cartouche, is lost.

matter the criminals adapted into the social-bandit pantheo
like Dick Turpin, Cartouche and Schinderhannes. Even in th
Balkans, where the recorded history of haiduks and klepht
goes back to the fifteenth century, the earliest klephtic hero
who survive as such in the Greek ballads seem to be Christo
Millionis (1740s) and Bukovallas, who flourished even later.
is inconceivable that men such as these should not have bee
the subjects of song and story earlier than this. Great briganc

insurgents like Marco Sciarra of the late sixteenth century must have had their legend, and at least one of the great bandits of that extremely disturbed period – Serralonga in Catalonia – did become a popular hero whose memory survived into the nineteenth century; but this case may be unusual. Why are most of them forgotten?

It is possible that there were some changes in the popular culture of western Europe which explain this efflorescence of bandit myths in the eighteenth century, but hard to account for what seems to be the similar chronology in eastern Europe. One might suggest that the memory of a purely oral culture – and those who perpetuated the fame of bandit-heroes were illiterate – is relatively short. Beyond a certain lapse of generations the memory of an individual merges with the collective picture of the legendary heroes of the past, the man with myth and ritual symbolism, so that a hero who happens to last beyond this span, like Robin Hood, can no longer be replaced in the context of real history. This is probably true, but not the whole truth. For oral memory can last longer than ten or twelve generations. Carlo Levi records that the peasants of the Basilicata in the 1930s remembered two episodes of history vividly though vaguely as 'their own': the time of the brigands seventy years ago, and the time of the great Hohenstaufen emperors seven centuries earlier. The sad truth is probably that the heroes of remote times survive because they are not *only* the heroes of the peasants. The great emperors had their clerks, chroniclers and poets, they left huge monuments of stone, they represent not the inhabitants of some lost corner of the highlands (which happens to be like so many other lost corners), but states, empires, entire peoples. So Skanderberg and Marko Kraljevic survive from the Middle Ages in Albanian and Serbian epics, but Mihat the Herdsman and Juhasz Andras (Andras the Shepherd) against whom

> no gun has any power,
> the balls which the Pandurs aim against him
> he catches in his naked hand,[1]

disappear in time. The great bandit is stronger, more famous,
his name lives longer than the ordinary peasant's, but he is no
less mortal. He is immortal only because there will always be
some other Mihat or Andras to take his gun into the hills or
on to the wide plains.

The second peculiarity is more familiar.

Bandits belong to the peasantry. If the argument of this book
is accepted, they cannot be understood except in the context of
the sort of peasant society which, it is safe to guess, is as remote
from most readers as ancient Egypt, and which is as surely
doomed by history as the Stone Age. Yet the curious and
astonishing fact about the bandit *myth* is that its appeal has
always been far wider than its native environment. German
literary historians have invented a special literary category, the
*Räuberromantik* ('bandit romanticism') which has produced a
large and by no means only Germanic supply of *Räuberromane*
('bandit novels'), none of them designed for reading by either
peasants or bandits. The purely fictional bandit-hero, a Rinaldo
Rinaldini or Joaquin Murieta, is its characteristic by-product.
But more remarkable still, the bandit-hero survives the modern
industrial revolution of culture, to appear, in his original
form in television series about Robin Hood and his merry
men, in a more modern version as the Western or gangster
hero, in the mass media of the late twentieth century urban
life.

That the official culture of countries in which social banditry
is endemic, should reflect its importance, is natural. Cervantes
put the celebrated Spanish robbers of the late sixteenth century
into his works, as naturally as Walter Scott wrote about Rob
Roy. Hungarian, Rumanian, Czechoslovak and Turkish writers
devote novels to real or imaginary bandit-heroes, while – a
slight twist – a modernizing Mexican novelist anxious to dis-
credit the myth, attempts to cut the hero down to size of
ordinary criminals in *Los Bandidos del Rio Frio*.* In such

---

* I am thinking of Zsigmond Moricz's novel about Sandor Rósza, Panait
Istrati's *Les Haidoucs*, Yashar Kemal's *Mehmed My Hawk*, and above all
the remarkable *Der Räuber Nikola Schuhaj* of the Czech Ivan Olbracht.

ountries both bandits and bandit myths are important facts of
fe, impossible to overlook.

The bandit myth is also comprehensible in highly urbanized
ountries which still possess a few empty spaces of 'outback' or
vest' to remind them of a sometimes imaginary heroic past,
nd to provide a concrete *locus* for nostalgia, a symbol of
ncient and lost virtue, a spiritual Indian territory for which,
ke Huckleberry Finn, man can imagine himself 'lighting out'
hen the constraints of civilization become too much for him.
here the outlaw and bushranger Ned Kelly still rides, as in
e paintings of the Australian Sidney Nolan, a ghostly figure,

1. Contemporary impression of Ned Kelly (1854–80) in his
rmour.

agic, menacing and fragile in his home-made armour, crossing
nd re-crossing the sun-bleached Australian hinterland, waiting
or death.

Nevertheless there is more to the literary or popular cultural
nage of the bandit than the documentation of contemporary
fe in backward societies, the longing for lost innocence and
dventure in advanced ones. There is what remains when we
rip away the local and social framework of brigandage: a

permanent emotion and a permanent role. There is freedom heroism, and the dream of justice.

The myth of Robin Hood stresses the first and the third these ideals. What survives from the medieval greenwood t appear on the television screen is the fellowship of free an equal men, the invulnerability to authority, and the cham pionship of the weak, oppressed and cheated. The classica version of the bandit myth in high culture insists on the sam elements. Schiller's robbers sing of the free life in the fores while their chief, the noble Karl Moor, gives himself up tha the reward for his capture can save a poor man. The Wester and the gangster film insist on the second, the heroic elemen even against the obstacle of conventional morality which con fines heroism to the good, or at least the morally ambiguou gunman. Yet there is no denying it. The bandit is brave, bot in action and as victim. He dies defiantly and well, and un numbered boys from slums and suburbs, who possess nothin but the common but nevertheless precious gift of strength an courage, can identify themselves with him. In a society in whic men live by subservience, as ancillaries to machines of metal o moving parts of human machinery, the bandit lives and die with a straight back. As we have seen, not every legendar bandit of history survives thus, to feed the dreams of urba frustration. In fact hardly any of the great bandits of histor survive the translation from agrarian to industrial society except when they are virtually contemporary with it, or whe they have already been embalmed in that resistant medium fo time-travel, literature. Chap-books about Lampião are printe today among the sky-scrapers of São Paulo, because every on of the millions of first generation migrants from the Brazilia north-east knows about the great *cangaçeiro* who was killed i 1938, i.e. in the actual lifetimes of all who are more than thirt years old. Contrariwise, twentieth-century Englishmen an Americans know about Robin Hood 'who took from the ric and gave to the poor' and twentieth-century Chinese about 'th Opportune Rain Sung Chiang … who helps the needy an looks lightly upon silver', because writing and printing trans

rmed a local and spoken tradition into a national and per-
anent form. One might say that the intellectuals have ensured
e survival of the bandits.

In a sense, they still do so today. The rediscovery of the social
andits in our time is the work of intellectuals – of writers, of
m-makers, even of historians. The book is part of the re-
scovery. It has tried to explain the phenomenon of social
anditry, but also to present heroes: Janošik, Sandor Rósza,
ovbuš, Doncho Vatach, Diego Corrientes, Jancu Jiano,
Iusolino, Giuliano, Bukovallas, Mihat the Herdsman, Andras
ie Shepherd, Santanon, Serralonga and Garcia, an endless
attle-order of warriors, swift as stags, noble as falcons, cun-
ing as foxes. Except for a few, nobody ever knew them thirty
iles from their place of birth, but they were as important to
ieir people as Napoleons or Bismarcks; almost certainly more
nportant than the real Napoleon and Bismarck. Nobody who
insignificant has several hundred songs made about him, like
anošik. They are songs of pride, and of longing:

> The cuckoo has called
> On the dry branch
> They have killed Shuhaj
> And times are hard now.[2]

For the bandits belong to remembered history, as distinct
om the official history of books. They are part of the history
hich is not so much a record of events and those who shaped
iem, as of the symbols of the theoretically controllable but
ctually uncontrolled factors which determine the world of the
oor: of just kings and men who bring justice to the people.
hat is why the bandit legend still has power to move us. Let us
ave the last word to Ivan Olbracht, who has written better
bout it than almost anyone else.

Ian has an insatiable longing for justice. In his soul he rebels
gainst a social order which denies it to him, and whatever the
orld he lives in, he accuses either that social order or the entire
iaterial universe of injustice. Man is filled with a strange, stubborn
rge to remember, to think things out and to change things; and in

addition he carries within himself the wish to have what he cann
have – if only in the form of a fairy tale. That is perhaps the ba
for the heroic sagas of all ages, all religions, all peoples and a
classes.[3]

Including ours. That is why Robin Hood is our hero to
and will remain so.

# Appendix:

# Women and Banditry

Since bandits are notoriously given to womanizing, and both pride and status require such demonstrations of virility, the most usual role of women in banditry is as lovers. Anti-social bandits can supplement their sexual attractions by rape, which in certain circumstances can guarantee that the victims will not talk. ('They said they were doing all this to us so that we would be too ashamed to talk, and to show what they were capable of,' a Colombian girl reported to the guerrillas she subsequently joined.[1] However, as Machiavelli observed long ago, interfering with women is a certain way to become unpopular, and bandits who rely on popular support or connivance must keep their instincts in check. The rule in Lampião's band was never to rape, ('except for good reasons', i.e. presumably for punishment, revenge and terror). Political peasant guerrillas apply this rule with the greatest rigour: 'We explain the rule: a guerrilla who rapes a woman, any woman, is court-martialled.' But, among both bandits and guerrillas 'If it's a natural thing, if the woman agrees, then there's no problem.'[2]

Characteristically, women are visited by their bandit-lovers, a fact which facilitates de facto polygyny. But cases of girls sharing the roving life of the men are not unknown, though bands which systematically allow this practice are probably rare. Lampião's seems to have been the only one in north-east Brazil. Even so, when the men went on a particularly long and dangerous expedition they preferred to leave the women behind, often against their will, since the presence of a man's girl would inhibit his casual amorous adventures 'out of respect for the regular companion'.[3]

The women in a band would not normally step outside their accepted sexual role. They carried no firearms, and normally took no part in the fighting. Maria Bonita, Lampião's wife embroidered, sewed, cooked, sang, danced and had children in the middle of the bush.... She was satisfied to follow her husband. When necessary she took part in the fighting, but in general she merely looked on, urging her husband not to take too many risks.[4] However, Dadá, the wife of his lieutenant Corisco, had more of the Lady Macbeth in her, and could well have commanded a band herself. There are obvious inconveniences in having what is virtually always a small minority of women in a band of men. Fear of a redoubtable chief can minimize them, or in groups with the high political conscious-ness of peasant guerrillas, the disciplined morality of the cause. This may be the main reason for the reluctance of bandits to take women with them, or to interfere with women prisoners. Nothing saps solidarity as much as sexual rivalry.

The second and less publicized role of women in banditry is as supporters and links with the outside world. Mostly, it is to be presumed, they help kinsmen, husbands or lovers. Not much needs to be said about this.

The third role is as bandits themselves. Few women are active fighters, but enough cases occur in the balladry of the Balkan haiduks (see Chapter 5)[5] to make us suspect that they are at least in certain parts of the world a recognized phenomenon. In the Peruvian department of Piura, for instance, several flourished during the period 1917–1937, including some band-leaders; notably Rosa Palma from Chulucanas, who is said to have earned the respect even of the formidable Froilán Alama, the most famous chief of the time, the lesbian Rosa Ruirías from Morropón, a notably combative community, and Bárbara Ramos, sister of two bandits and com-panion of another, from the *hacienda* Huapalas.*[6] These girls were renowned as horsewomen, sharpshooters and for their bravery. Except for their sex, there seems to have been nothing to distinguish them from any other bandits.

A clue to this phenomenon may come from Andalusia, where such women-bandits are not only recorded (e.g. in the nineteenth-century Torralba of Lucena [who wore male dress] and Maria Márquez Zafra [La Marimacho]), but also occupy a special place in the bandit legend as *serranas* (mountain women).[8] The stereotypical *serrana* turns to outlawry in general and revenge on men in par-ticular, because she has been 'dishonoured', i.e. deflowered. Such an activist reaction to dishonour is no doubt relatively even rarer among women than among men, but champions of the more militant type of women's liberation may be gratified to note that even traditional societies recognize it. However, like so much about banditry, this subject awaits further research.

*Nothing is known of their fate, and they are not recorded in the list of bandits arrested and killed in this area,[7] though this list contains some other women.

In so far as they are avenged, most 'dishonoured' women in the societies breeding banditry are likely to find champions in their menfolk. Defence of 'honour', i.e. largely the sexual 'honour' of women, is probably the most important single motive that has led men into outlawry in the classical bandit regions of the Mediterranean and the overseas Latin world. The bandit there combined the functions both of the Statue and of Don Juan; but in this, as in so many other respects, he shared the values of his social universe.

# Bibliography

PREFACES

1 Charles Macfarlane, *The Lives and exploits of* banditi *and robbers in all parts of the world*, London, 1833.
2 (Anon.) *Chucho El Roto o la nobleza de un bandido mexicano*, Mexico, 1963, p. 68.


CHAPTER 1

1 Molise, quoted in F. Molfese, *Storia del brigantaggio dopo l'unità*, Milan, 1964, p. 131.
2 Calculated on the basis of G. Guzman, O. Fals Borda, E. Umaña Luna, *La Violencia en Colombia*, Bogota, 1964, II, pp. 287–97.
3 *Le brigandage en Macédoine: Un rapport confidentiel au gouvernement bulgare*, Berlin, 1908, p. 38; information from Professor D. Dakin of Birkbeck College.
4 D. Eeckhaute, 'Les brigands en Russie du dix-septième au dix-neuvième siècle' in *Rev. Hist. Mod. and Contemp.* XII, 1965, pp. 174–5.
5 E. Alabaster, *Notes and commentaries on the Chinese, criminal law*, Luzak and Co., pp. 400–402.
6 E. Lopez Albujar, *Los caballeros del delito*, Lima, 1936, p. 75–6.
7 W. Crooke, *The tribes and castes of the North-West Provinces and Oudhe*, Calcutta, 1896, 4 vols., 1, p. 49.
8 F. Molfese, op. cit., p. 130.
9 M. I. P. de Queiroz, *Os cangaçeiros: les bandits d'honneur brésiliens*, Paris, 1968, pp. 142, 164.
10 R. Rowland, ' "Cantadores" del nordeste brasileño' in *Aportes* 3 Jan. 1967, p. 138. For the real relations between this bandit and the holy man, which were rather more *nuancés*, cf. E. de Lima, *O mundo estranho dos cangaçeiros*, Salvador and Bahia, 1965, pp. 113–4 and O. Anselmo, *Padre Cicero*, Rio de Janeiro 1968.

CHAPTER 2

1  Autobiography in G. Rosen, *Die Balkan-Haiduken*, Leipzig, 1878, p. 78.

2  Molfese, op. cit., pp. 127–8.

3  Hobsbawm, *Primitive Rebels*, Manchester University Press, 1959; Lopez Albujar, op. cit., p. 126.

4  Alejandro Franco, 'El Aymara del siglo XX' in *Amauta* (Lima) 23, 1929, p. 88.

5  Based on Molfese, op. cit., pp. 367–82.

6  A. H. Smith, *Village life in China*, New York, Chicago and Toronto, 1899, pp. 213–17.

7  F. C. B. Avé-Lallemant, *Das deutsche Gaunerthum*, Leipzig, 1858–62, II, p. 91 n.

8  For details, G. Kraft, *Historische Studien zu Schillers Schauspiel 'Die Räuber'*, Weimar, 1959.

9  Avé-Lallemant, op. cit., I, 241. For confirmation of the differences between criminals and bandits from a medico-legal expert with experience of both, E. de Lima, op. cit., *passim*; G. Sangnier, *Le brigandage dans le Pas-de-Calais*, Blangermont, 1962, pp. 172, 196.


CHAPTER 3

1  Pearl Buck (translator), *All men are brothers*, New York, 1937, p. 1258.

2  E. Morselli and S. de Sanctis, *Biografia di un bandito: Giuseppe Musolino, di fronte alla psichiatra ed alla sociologia*, Milan n.d., p. 175.

3  C. Bernaldo de Quiros, *El bandolerismo en España y Mexico*, Mexico, 1959, p. 59.

4  M. Pavlovich, 'Zelim Khan et le brigandage au Caucase' in *Rev. du monde musulman* XX, 1912, pp. 144, 146.

5  V. Zapata Cesti, *La delincuencia en el Peru*, Lima n.d., p. 175.

6  M. L. Guzman, *The memoirs of Pancho Villa*, Austin, 1965, p. 8.

7  Alberto Carrillo Ramirez, *Luis Pardo, 'El Gran Bandido'*, Lima, 1970, pp. 117–8, 121.

8  Miguel Barnet, *Cimarrón*, Havana, 1967, p. 87–8.

9  R. V. Russell, *The tribes and castes of the Central Provinces of India*, Macmillan, 1916, 4 vols, I, p. 60; Charles Hervey, *Some records of crime*, Simpson, 1892, I, p. 331.

10 Kent L. Steckmesser, 'Robin Hood and the American outlaw' in *Journal of American folklore*, 79, April–June 1966, p. 350.

11 Pearl Buck (translator), op. cit., p. 328.

12 J. Martinez-Alier, *La Estabilidad del latifundismo*, Paris, 1968, chapters 1–6.

13 J. Caro Baroja, *Ensayo sobre la leteratura de Cordel*, Madrid, 1969, p. 375.

14 A. v. Schweiger-Lerchenfeld, *Bosnien*, Vienna, 1878, p. 122; P. Bourde, *En Corse*, Paris, 1887, p. 218–19.

15 I take all this information from Douglas Dakin's *The Greek struggle in Macedonia*, Salonica, 1966.

16 F. Kanitz, *La Bulgarie danubienne*, Paris, 1882, p. 346.

17 Special number on Calabria of *Il Ponte*, 1950, p. 1305.

18 Juan Regla Campistol and Joan Fuster, *El bandolerisme català*, Barcelona, 1963, II, p. 35.

19 D. H. Meijer, 'Over het bendewezen op Java' in *Indonesie* III, 1949–50, p. 183; Crooke, op. cit., p. 47. See also Nertan Macedo, *Capitão Virgulino Ferreira da Silva: Lampiao*, 2nd edn., Rio de Janeiro, 1968, p. 96.

20 Ivan Olbracht, *Der Räuber Nikola Schuhaj*, East Berlin, 1953, p. 100.

21 C. G. Harper, *Half-hours with the highwaymen*, London, 1908, II, p. 235.

CHAPTER 4

1 Antonio Teodoro dos Santos, 'Lampiao, king of the bandits' in *O poeta Garimpeiro*, chapbook, Sao Paulo, 1959.

2 Nertan Macedo, op. cit., p. 183.

3 cf. Paris Lozano, 'Los guerilleros del Tolima' in *Revista de las Indias*, Bogota, 1936, I, no. 4, p. 31.

4 Y. Kemal, *Mehmed My hawk*, Collins, 1961, p. 56.

5 Guzman, Fals Borda, Umaña Luna, op. cit., I, p. 182.

6 ibid, II, pp. 327–8.

7 Ivan Olbracht, *Berge und Jahrhunderte*, East Berlin, 1952, pp. 82–3.

CHAPTER 5

1 From A. Dozon, *Chansons populaires bulgares inédites*, Paris, 1875, p. 208.

2  A. Strausz, *Bulgarische Volksdichtungen*, Vienna and Leipzig, 1895, pp. 295–7.

3  *Le brigandage en Macédoine*, loc cit., p. 37. For the absence of homosexuality among Brazilian bandits, E. de Lima, op cit., p. 45.

4  A. Dozon, op. cit., p. 184.

5  J. Baggalay, *Klephtic ballads*, Blackwell, 1936, pp. 18–19; C. J. Jireček, *Geschichte der Bulgaren*, Prague, 1876, p. 474.

6  J. C. V. Engel, *Staatskunde und Geschichte von Dalmatien, Croatien und Slavonien*, Halle, 1798, p. 232.

7  Marko Fedorowitsch, *Die Slawen der Türkei*, Dresden and Leipzig, 1844, II, p. 206.


CHAPTER 6

1  J. Usang Ly, in *Journal of Race Development* 8, 1917–18, p. 370.

2  Leonardo Mota, *No tempo de Lampião*, Rio de Janeiro, 1968 edn., pp. 55–6.

3  M. I. P. de Queiroz, op. cit., pp. 9–10.

4  Leonardo Mota, op. cit., p. 54.

5  R. V. Russell, op. cit., I, pp. 52–3; III, pp. 237–9, 474.

6  *See* O. Anselmo, op. cit., pp. 528–36.

7  *See* Teniente Coronel (R) Genaro Matos, *Operaciones irregulares al norte de Cajamarca 1924–5 a 1927*, Lima, 1968.

8  Romulo Merino Arana, *Historia policial del Peru*, Lima n.d., pp. 177–8; G. Matos, op. cit., p. 390–98.

9  G. Matos, op. cit., p. 75; cited from Salamón Vilchez Murga, *Fusiles y Machetes*, a local source.

10  D. Eeckhaute, loc. cit., pp. 201–2.


CHAPTER 7

1  J. Delumeau, *Vie économique et sociale de Rome dans la seconde moitié du seizième* siècle, Paris, 1957–9, II, p. 557.

2  P. M. van Wulfften-Palthe, *Psychological aspects of the Indonesian problem*, Leiden, 1949, p. 32.

3  J. Koetschet, *Aus Bosniens letzter Türkenzeit*, Vienna and Leipzig, 1905, pp. 6–8.

4  *District gazetteers of the United Provinces*, Allahabad 1911, I, p. 185.

5  Sartono Kartodirdjo, *The peasants' revolt of Banten in 1888*, Hague, 1966, p. 23.
6  Wulfften-Palthe, op. cit., p. 34.
7  Pavlovich, loc. cit., pp. 146, 159.
8  cf. M. L. Guzman, op. cit.
9  Stuart Schram, *Mao Tse-tung*, Penguin, 1966, p. 43.
10  Luis Gonzalez, *Pueblo en vilo*, Mexico DF, 1968, p. 251.

CHAPTER 8

1  E. Lister, 'Lessons of the Spanish Guerilla War (1939–51)' in *World Marxist Review* 8, II, 1965, pp. 53–8; Tomas Cossias, *La lucha contra el 'Maquis' en España*, Madrid, 1956.

CHAPTER 9

1  A. J. Paterson, *The Magyars: their country and institutions*, London, 1869, I, p. 213.
2  I. Olbracht, *Berge and Jahrhunderte*, p. 113.
3  I. Olbracht, *Der Räuber Nikola Schuhaj*, pp. 76–7.

APPENDIX

1  *Diario de un guerillero Latinamericano*, Montevideo, 1968, p. 60.
2  ibid., pp. 60–61.
3  M. I. P. de Queiroz, op. cit., p. 179.
4  ibid, p. 183.
5  C. J. Jireček, op. cit., p. 476.
6  V. Zapata Cesti, op. cit., pp. 205–6.
7  In R. Merino Arana, op. cit.
8  Julio Caro Baroja discusses them, op. cit., pp. 389–90.

# Further Reading

There are few general discussions of social banditry besides a chapter in E. J. Hobsbawm, *Primitive rebels*, Manchester University Press 1959. In the absence of comparative studies we must turn to national and regional monographs. For ITALY, whose *banditi* were long the most famous in (foreign) literature and art we probably possess more monographs than for any other country; cf. the eighteen-page bibliography in F. Ferracuti, R. Lazzari, M. E. Wolfgang, *Violence in Sardinia*, Rome 1970, which deals with only one region. F. Molfese, *Storia del brigantaggio dopo l'Unità*, Milan, 1964, esp. part I, chapter 3, and Enzo d'Alessandro, *Brigantaggio e mafia in Sicilia*, Messina and Firenze 1959, are to be recommended. For SPAIN, Juan Regla Campistol and Joan Fuster, *El bandolerisme català*, Barcelona 1962–1963, and C. Bernaldo de Quiros, *El bandolerismo en Espana y Mexico*, Mexico 1959, are helpful. In LATIN AMERICA some countries are unusually well supplied with bandit studies, notably PERU and BRAZIL. For the former, E. Lopez Albujar, *Los Caballeros del delito*, Lima 1936, – see also the same author's *Cuentos Andinos* (various editions), J. Varallanos, *Bandoleros en el Peru*, Lima 1937, and a number of more esoteric studies by policemen and soldiers, all unfortunately, like most Peruvian publications, extremely hard to find. For the latter, fortunately Maria Isaura Pereira de Queiroz, *Os Cangaçeiros, les bandits d'honneur brésiliens*, Paris 1968, contains all that most of us need to know about the bandits of the north-east.

EAST EUROPEAN banditry is discussed comparatively in I. Rácz, *Couches militaires issues de la paysannerie libre en Europe orientale du quinzième au dix-septième siècle*, Debreczen 1964. For RUSSIA, Denise Eeckhoute, 'Les brigands en Russie du dix-septième au dix-neuvième siècle: mythe et réalité' in *Rev. Hist. Mod. and Contemp.* XII, 1965, pp. 161–202. Philip Longworth, *The Cossacks* (Constable 1969) discusses a subject not unconnected with banditry. For BULGARIA, the old but invaluable Georg Rosen, *Die Balkan-Haiduken*, Leipzig 1878, and B. Tsvetkova, 'Mouvements anti-féodaux dans les terres bulgares ... du seizième au dix-huitième siècle', in *Etudes Historiques*, Sofia 1965; for BOSNIA, A. V. Schweiger-Lerchenfeld, *Bosnien*, Vienna 1878, for SERBIA, G. Castellan, *La vie quotidienne en Serbie au seuil de l'indépendance*,

Paris 1967. For CARPATHO-UKRAINE, Ivan Olbracht's reportage *Berge und Jahrhunderte*, East Berlin 1952, the raw material for his wonderful novel (see below). Readers should be warned that no adequate study of East European banditry is possible without a knowledge of the local languages.

For ASIAN banditry, Jean Chesneaux, *Les sociétés secrètes chinoises*, Paris 1965 has a chapter on the subject; see also K.-C. Hsiao, *Rural China*, Seattle 1960. Sartono Kartodirdjo, *The Peasants' Revolt of Banten in 1888*, Leiden 1888, and P. M. van Wulfften-Palthe, *Psychological Aspects of the Indonesian Problem*, Leiden 1949 deal with JAVA. R. V. Russell, *The Tribes and Castes of the Central Provinces of India*, 4 vols Macmillan 1916, may serve as a specimen of the most accessible sources for dacoity.

As for banditry in the 'developed' countries, the Robin Hood problem is discussed in *Past and Present*, nos. 14, 18, 19, 20 (1958, 1960–1) by R. H. Hilton, J. C. Holt, M. Keen and T. H. Aston; Mandrin in F. Funck-Brentano, *Mandrin*, Paris 1908, without much insight. On the other hand F. C. B. Avé-Lallemant, *Das Deutsche Gaunerthum*, 4 vols, Leipzig 1858–62 is a comprehensive introduction to the pre-industrial underworld. Of the large North American literature on outlaws, we need mention only Kent L. Steckmesser, 'Robin Hood and the American Outlaw', in *Journal of American Folklore* 79, 1966, no. 312, which provides a basis for comparisons and contains bibliographical references.

We are fortunate to possess several biographies, autobiographies and documentary novels about or by bandits. Panayot Hitov's memoirs are in G. Rosen, op. cit. M. L. Guzman, *Memorias de Pancho Villa*, Mexico, numerous editions, are translated *con brio* as *The Memoirs of Pancho Villa*, Austin 1965. Alberto Carrillo Ramirez, *Luis Pardo 'El Gran Bandido', vida y hechos del famoso bandolero chiquiano que acaparó la atención publica durante varios anos*, Lima 1970, deals with the classical 'noble bandit' of Peru, and contains numerous anecdotes and ballads. F. Cascella, *Il brigantaggio, ricerche sociologiche e antropologiche*, Aversa 1907, includes an autobiography of Crocco; E. Morsello and S. De Sanctis, *Biografia di unban dito: Giuseppe Musolino*, Milan n.d., is another of the products of the same school of Italian criminology. There are various lives and reminiscences of Sardinian bandits, cf. the bibliography cited above. Estacio de Lima, *O mundo estranho dos can-*

*gaçeiros,* Salvador-Bahia 1965, contains substantial memoirs by Angelo Roque; M. I. P. de Queiroz op. cit., other first-hand statements by Brazilian bandits. Though some of these sources are virtually unobtainable, they are mentioned here, because bandits are seldom heard speaking in their own voices. Gavin Maxwell, *God Protect Me from My Friends,* Pan 1957, is about Giuliano.

Among the numerous bandit novels, by far the best I know is *Der Räuber Nikola Schuhaj,* East Berlin 1953, German trans. from the Czech. Other revealing novels – among the many on this topic – are Yashar Kemal, *Mehmed My Hawk,* Harvin Press and Collins 1961, an introduction to Turkish banditry, and the famous *Shui Hu Chuan* (Water Margin Novel), translated by Pearl Buck as *All Men are Brothers,* New York 1937, essential reading for Chinese banditry. E. About's *Le Roi des Montagnes* is a disenchanted picture of post-liberation Greek brigandage; Walter Scott's *Rob Roy* (with a useful historical introduction) is much less misleading about its subject than the same author's *Ivanhoe* is about Robin Hood.

Bandits have been the subjects of numerous films. None of these has value as a historical source, but at least two add greatly to our understanding of the bandit environment: V. de Seta's *Banditi ad Orgosolo* and Francesco Rosi's masterly *Salvatore Giuliano.*

It is impossible to study the legends and songs of banditry in West-European languages, but G. Rosen, op. cit., A. Dozon, *Chansons populaires bulgares inédites,* Paris 1875, Adolf Strausz, *Bulgarische Volksdichtungen,* Vienna and Leipzig 1895, give a reasonable selection of haiduk ballads, while John Baggalay, *Klephtic Ballads,* Blackwell 1936, and B. Knös, *Histoire de la Littérature Néo-Grecque,* Uppsala 1962, introduce the much less revealing Greek ones. What linguistic ignorance debars us from, may be indicated by the English summary of J. Horak and K. Plicka, *Zbojnicke piesne slovenskoho l'udu,* Bratislava 1963, which contains 700 songs about bandits, all from Slovakia. There are few scholarly studies of the bandit legend. Joan Fuster, *El bandolerisme català,* vol. II, is the fullest I know. M. I. P. de Queiroz, op. cit., deals briefly with the contemporary development of the *cangaçeiro* myth in Brazil since about 1950. Julio Caro Baroja, *Ensayo Sobre la Leteratura de Cordel,* Madrid 1969, Chapter XVIII, deals very fully with the popular literature on banditry in Spain, and incidentally contains important data and reflections on the phenomenon in that country.

# Index of Bandits

# General Index

## Penguinews and
## Penguins in Print

Our illustrated magazine *Penguinews* appears every
month; it contains details of all the latest Penguins,
Pelicans and Puffins.

*Penguinews* always contains an article on a major
author, plus many other items of interest.

To supplement *Penguinews* we have *Penguins in
Print*, a complete list of all available Penguin titles
... there are now over four thousand to choose
from.

We can send you a free copy of the current
*Penguinews*, if you like.

And if you want to receive both publications
regularly just send us 30p (if you live in the United
Kingdom) or 60p (if you live elsewhere), for a year's
issues. A cheque or a postal order will do.

Write to Dept EP, Penguin Books Ltd,
Harmondsworth, Middlesex, and we'll add your
name to our mailing list.

Note: *Penguinews* and *Penguins in Print* are not
available in the U.S.A. or Canada

# Gladiators

Michael Grant

'Professor Grant's monograph of one of the more revolting institutions of ancient Rome is an admirable piece of scholarship and welcome as filling out our knowledge of this neglected side of the Romans.

'Gladiatorial displays were . . . in origin part of the funeral rites of a dead warrior, but by the classical period this aspect had been largely forgotten and they were there to satisfy the baser nature of the Roman mob. The story is told in four chapters: Gladiators in Republican Rome, The Gladiators' Profession, Gladiators in Action, and The Gladiators and their Public. It is a thoroughly readable, straightforward and complete account, well documented by reference to contemporary sources and copiously illustrated' – *The Times Educational Supplement*

'*Gladiators* is a crisp, comprehensive and thoroughly readable monograph, which handles its sources with intelligent discretion' – *The Times Literary Supplement*

Bandits—p. 160

Also by E. J. Hobsbawm

# Industry and Empire

*The Pelican Economic History of Britain Volume 3*

The industrial revolution marks the most fundamenta
transformation in the history of the world recorded in
written documents. For a brief period it coincided with the
history of a single country, Great Britain. This book
describes and accounts for Britain's rise as the world's first
industrial world power, its decline from the temporary
dominance of the pioneer, its rather special relationship
with the rest of the world (notably the underdeveloped
countries), and the effects of all these on the life of the
British people.

'When a brilliantly gifted and learned man impatiently sets
about the lesser people who profess his subject, he writes a
book that attracts and deserves attention. Eric Hobsbawm,
by far the most gifted economic historian now writing, has
done just this. Under the guise of a textbook he has
produced an original and masterly reinterpretation of
Western economic (not to speak of social and political)
history' – John Vaizey in the *Listener*

'A masterly survey of the major economic developments
and changes of the last 200 years, sharply and ironically
observed, elegantly written and, for the statistically
undernourished, illustrated by a host of excellent diagrams
and maps' – *Guardian*